LEADING
ON PURPOSE

LEADING
ON PURPOSE

Sage Advice *and* Practical Tools
for Becoming *the* Complete Leader

TIMOTHY I. THOMAS & CHARLES "RIP" TILDEN

GREENLEAF
BOOK GROUP PRESS

Published by Greenleaf Book Group Press
Austin, Texas
www.gbgpress.com

Copyright ©2014 Makarios Consulting, LLC

Distributed by Greenleaf Book Group

For ordering information or special discounts for bulk purchases, please contact Greenleaf Book Group at PO Box 91869, Austin, TX 78709, 512.891.6100.

Design and composition by Greenleaf Book Group
Cover design by Greenleaf Book Group
Cover Illustration: Branchegevara/iStock Collection/Thinkstock

Cataloging-in-Publication data
Thomas, Timothy I.
   Leading on purpose : sage advice and practical tools for becoming the complete leader / Timothy I. Thomas & Charles "Rip" Tilden.—First edition.
      pages : illustrations ; cm
   Issued also as an ebook.
   Includes bibliographical references and index.
   1. Leadership. 2. Management. 3. Strategic planning. 4. Personnel management. 5. Organizational change. I. Tilden, Charles, 1953- II. Title.
HD57.7 .T46 2014
658.4/092   2014938338

ISBN 13: 978-1-62634-127-2

Part of the Tree Neutral® program, which offsets the number of trees consumed in the production and printing of this book by taking proactive steps, such as planting trees in direct proportion to the number of trees used: www.treeneutral.com

TreeNeutral®

Printed in the United States of America on acid-free paper

14 15 16 17 18 19   10 9 8 7 6 5 4 3 2 1

First Edition
eBook ISBN: 978-1-62634-128-9

Dedication

In memory of Robert E. Maloney, friend, mentor, and father figure who blessed me in immeasurable ways in both my personal and professional life. I miss our Friday afternoon calls where I learned so much about leadership and life. —Tim

For my wife, Beth, my best friend and the love of my life. Her love, laughter, and never-ending commitment to our journey together have inspired me since the day I fell in love with her. To our children, Matt, Emily, and Mike, who, together, with their spouses, Emily, Mansoor, and Lauran, have taught us why faith and family matter most in our lives. That tradition continues with our five beautiful grandchildren: Joshua, Kieran, Humza, Zahra, and Cecilia. —Rip

ACKNOWLEDGMENTS

We want to acknowledge a wonderfully talented group of professionals who played an important role in helping us develop this book. We were blessed to work with Paula Marolewski whose sharp questions, good counsel, and ability to turn a phrase were invaluable to the text of the book. We are grateful to Hilary Hinzmann, an insightful and demanding editor whose commitment to excellence strengthened our writing. We also offer our sincere thanks to Gene Schultz, who designed the illustrations and diagrams. We are blessed by the long-standing support, attention to detail, and friendship of Paige Infortuna, our tireless executive administrator. We also wish to acknowledge the many passionate and courageous clients over the years who have taught us much about leadership and whose wisdom can be found in the pages of this book. Finally, we had a great deal of fun writing this book and we want to acknowledge the laughs, insights, and inspiration we have shared with other each as business partners and friends.

CONTENTS

Introduction

FROM RANDOM WALK TO PURPOSEFUL JOURNEY: ACQUIRING LEADERSHIP SKILLS

Frustration. It's a common experience whether you are a CEO, VP, middle manager, or line supervisor. You feel the tension mounting—in your head, in your chest, in your gut—every time you

- see a lack of alignment and cohesion in your team,
- realize messages aren't flowing from the top down, or from the bottom up,
- cannot seem to move work off your desk,
- struggle to motivate disengaged employees,
- keep going over the same ground again and again with no resolution, or
- experience employee resistance to change.

The list could go on and on. The bottom line is this: you are frustrated because you aren't achieving the extraordinary results you *know* are within your reach.

We understand your frustration. We've seen it hundreds of times in our work with clients at Makarios Consulting, where we collaborate with men and women who are leading businesses of all sizes to improve business strategy, enhance the effectiveness of operations, strengthen leadership teams, and help to manage change. And we want to affirm one thing right at the start: extraordinary results *are* within your reach. This book is about helping you overcome the obstacles that are causing you frustration so you can accomplish the extraordinary.

But what is the root of this frustration? What is the common denominator of the difficulties you face on a day-to-day basis?

In its simplest terms, the problem is this: most businesspeople know how to *manage their business* down to the last product requirement and decimal place, but they don't know how to *lead their people* with the same degree of sophistication.

Consider the CEOs, COOs, VPs, managers, supervisors, and directors in today's typical company. How did most of these people get into their current roles? The vast majority of them have their current title because of their technical knowledge and/or organizational abilities. They have experience, qualifications, knowledge, and track records of success as individual performers, so companies promoted them into management positions. They know the work, and they know the business.

What these highly qualified individuals often do not have is sufficient experience in leading others to achieve demanding goals. Yes, they themselves are star performers. Yes, they have worked with others throughout their careers. But performing a task while working with people is vastly different from leading people effectively day by day. We have observed that star performers often race ahead of the people problems they leave in their wake, until they reach a point where their continued success depends on leadership skills they do not possess.

Perhaps you have experienced this yourself. It may be why you're reading this book now. You were a top performer. Then one day you were handed a promotion and a team to lead—or a team vastly bigger and more varied than you'd led in the past. Your job description changed overnight. You are now in a role that demands more than your efforts alone. How do you motivate your people, communicate with them, help them solve problems, lead them through change—and handle all the other challenges you will face as their leader? The fact of the matter is that without sophisticated people skills, you can have all the technical expertise in the world, but you won't be able to engage others to accomplish extraordinary results.

The TOP model helps us see this principle visually. Picture your company as a stool. If you have only Technical and Organizational skills, the stool has two legs and will fall over. A third leg is needed to make the stool stable: People skills.

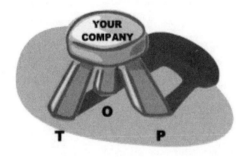

Technical skill is product and service know-how. *Organizational skill* means you can complete projects on time, on budget, and with the highest quality. But *people skills* make things happen.

Consider the facts. Do new leaders get the training they need to manage the people they are responsible for? Typically, the answer is no. "Congratulations, you're promoted! Good luck!" is the unfortunate reality. This is a serious problem. Most of the leaders who quit, are demoted, or are asked to leave a company do so because of a lack of people skills. You see the lack of people skills every day when

- feedback situations turn ugly,
- delegated responsibilities fall through the cracks,
- employees refer to their jobs as "the daily grind,"
- minor irritations become major roadblocks, or when
- great performers leave the company.

The problem is not with *who* is being promoted. Let us say it again: people are usually promoted into management roles or given greater management responsibilities because they are intelligent, hardworking, experienced, and business-savvy. The problem is the *lack of leadership training*. Just as it is difficult to gain technical knowledge and organizational expertise without training, it's also difficult to gain people skills without training. You have to work much harder at it.

A thought might be tickling your mind right now: "Wait a minute— isn't good leadership a character trait? Aren't some people 'natural-born leaders'? Isn't it true that you either have it or you don't?"

No, no, and no. Some people are more charismatic than others. But charisma is not a prerequisite to becoming an effective leader. A person can be charismatic but unable to strategize, resolve conflicts, effect change, lead a team to create a shared vision, or execute to deliver superior, sustainable results.

Leadership is not genetic. Doctors do not announce in the delivery room, "This baby has phenomenal leadership DNA!"

Leadership is a skill. And like all skills, it can be taught and it can be learned.

So how do people learn to lead? First, let's take a look at how we tend to learn—what we call the "random walk" approach. Then, let's look at a more effective and purposeful method, the way we *should* learn.

The Random Walk

Most of us learn to lead by negative example. Because there are more poor managers than good managers, chances are that you have seen a plethora of things you *don't* want to do. You may have been on the receiving end of suffocating micromanagement, experienced the consequences of shoddy communication, or been frustrated by a total lack of feedback. As a result, you made the commitment to yourself, "If I ever get a chance to lead, I'm certainly not going to do *that!*"

Once in a leadership role, you realize that you know what you don't want to do, but you aren't exactly sure what you should be doing instead. You know you resented not getting any feedback about your performance, but you don't know how to give feedback effectively to your staff now, especially when there are poor behavior patterns you want to change. You remember that a former director never delegated to anyone and was overworked to the point of a physical breakdown. You don't want that to happen to you, but you don't know what to delegate and who can handle various responsibilities.

So you try different techniques that you observed others use, or that you read about, or that you learned in a one-day seminar. This approach is haphazard at best. Some methods work. Many don't. A few have catastrophic results. And all the while, your frustration grows as you struggle to deliver on your commitments and to ensure that your team meets its deliverables. When it comes to your abilities as a leader, you are engaged in a random walk, and you know it.

A random walk may get you where you want to go, or it may not. But even if you do achieve your goals, you will have worked much harder than you needed to, and you won't be confident that you can repeat your results.

The Purposeful Journey

Over the years, we have talked with many excellent, skilled leaders. When we asked them about their leadership styles and how they developed as leaders, they all said essentially the same thing. They treated the development of their leadership skills very seriously. They took the opportunity to learn from experts, to study best practices, to attend seminars, and to constantly practice what they learned until they "got it right." They showed the same dedication as athletes training for a competition, or musicians rehearsing for a demanding performance.

Also, just like athletes and musicians, the great leaders we have known never assumed they had "arrived." They were continuous learners, always seeking new ways to improve and refine their skills. They demonstrated that there is a level of humility that is essential for great leadership: you have to be willing to listen, really hear what is being said, process it, and accept the fact that *you* may need to change. This is what we call "leading on purpose." It's the intentional development of your leadership skills, which this book is designed to help you pursue.

By making a commitment to purposeful, intentional, humble, and continuous learning, you will reduce the randomness of your walk and accelerate your growth as a leader. You will not be part of the majority who are pressured out of the leadership positions they have rightfully attained, but rather part of the smaller group of leaders who succeed and lead their teams to perform at a consistently high level.

It doesn't matter who you are: a supervisor or a CEO, a newly promoted manager, or a veteran of corporate business. You can put a stop to the random walk and take your first step on a purposeful journey.

What You'll Get from This Book

This book is a roadmap for your purposeful journey to becoming a complete leader—one who is able to excel in each of the skills we describe in the following chapters. Each chapter is laser-focused on one key area of leadership: style, strategy, communication, motivation, feedback, conflict resolution, execution, and change management.

Through every chapter, *you will deepen your knowledge and understanding of how leadership really works.* You will find key lessons about human behaviors, thought patterns, interactions, and motivations. You will discover the finest in leadership models and researched theory, not the "latest and greatest" fads. After all, your business is no place to test out the most recent pop psychology and hope it works. We've seen the value of the principles contained within these pages hundreds of times, in many industries, at all levels of leadership.

We offer you a solid theoretical grounding because, to quote the old saying, in order to build high, you have to dig deep. Theory is the foundation. It makes change both possible and sustainable. When you understand the principles, you will understand why the tools we provide work—and why they won't work if you don't apply them properly. Theory also enables you to apply the tools in virtually any circumstance—because you truly understand the concepts that are in play.

As your knowledge deepens and expands, *you will become more self-aware*. You'll better understand yourself—as a leader, as an individual, as a team member. You will be asked to take a hard look at yourself and at your interactions with others. Sometimes, what you see may be a little embarrassing. Occasionally, it may be downright rough. That's all right. With self-awareness comes the opportunity for positive change.

Finally, *you will get a full toolbox*. We believe that if information isn't rubber-meets-the-road practical, then it's useless. We're going to give you real tools to get real results in your leadership responsibilities. The tools aren't difficult to understand, though they will take practice to use skillfully. Don't give up. Keep working at them. These are skills, and skills must be learned and honed over time. Mistakes are part of the learning process. Time and effort *will* make these skills second nature to you, enabling you to consistently achieve extraordinary results.

We have more good news: you won't be alone on this journey. We want to show you how these principles and tools work, not just explain them to you. So you'll have two people beside you every step of the way: Frank Abernathy, CEO of a telecommunications firm, and his sharp-eyed, sometimes sharp-tongued, but always sagacious grandmother. As you witness Frank's struggles—similar to those every leader faces—and his grandmother's refreshingly candid spin on how he can meet them, we hope that you'll see the tools and theory come to life.

A Glimpse of Your Destination

Take a deep breath. Before you begin, we want to give you a glimpse of your destination. This is what *your* work environment will be like once you make the skills in this book your own and become the complete leader. Imagine for a minute that you're doing the following on a regular basis:

- Skillfully interacting with people to achieve trust, engagement, and alignment. That's effective **leadership style** (chapter 1).

- Creatively developing a set of clear, measurable goals and a shared vision for your company. That's focused **strategy** (chapter 2).

- Effectively transmitting ideas and facilitating input across all levels of the organization. That's powerful **communication** (chapter 3).

- Proactively fashioning an environment that produces engaged employees and increased commitment. That's inspiring **motivation** (chapter 4).

- Dramatically reducing poor performance and increasing productivity. That's the result of effective **feedback** (chapter 5).

- Assertively entering tense situations with the assurance that you can turn the issue into an opportunity for growth. That's courageous **conflict resolution** (chapter 6).

- Consistently improving daily operations, output, and profitability. That's focused **execution** (chapter 7).

- Confidently helping the people around you embrace change more quickly with a positive attitude and outlook. That's transformational **change management** (chapter 8).

You can do all this, and do it well, once you're equipped with the concepts and tools in this book and have ended your random walk to lead on purpose. Along your leadership journey, you'll continue to hone each of these skills, increasing your effectiveness as a leader with every passing year. Now, without any further ado, let's meet Frank Abernathy and his grandmother as we explore our first topic: leadership style.

FOLLOW THE LEADER:
UNDERSTANDING LEADERSHIP STYLE

Frank Abernathy parked his car and turned off the ignition. And then he sat there, staring. Not staring at the pleasant home he had come to visit. Just staring at nothing. Staring at that place inside himself that was increasingly empty and barren.

Eventually he heaved a sigh, got out of the car, and trudged slowly up the walk. He gave a light knock and entered without waiting for a reply.

"Took you long enough, Frankie," said an amused voice that had lost none of its crispness in over eight decades of living.

Frankie. All day long he was "Mr. Abernathy," "Sir," "Mr. President," "the CEO." To a few he was "Frank," but even that was said with respect. But right now—more than anything else—he wanted to be "Frankie."

"Sorry, Grandma. Just thinking." He removed his coat and hat and loosened his tie.

His grandmother watched him shrewdly from her favorite La-Z-Boy by the bay window. The bulk of the chair seemed to dwarf her compact frame. "Not pleasant thoughts."

"No."

"Well, then?"

Frank wandered into the kitchen and drew himself a glass of water. He wandered back to the living room. His grandmother was still watching him. "I'm founder, president, and CEO of a telecommunications firm that has an outstanding product," *he said, almost bitterly.* "Everyone wants what we've got! So why can't we move forward?"

"Well, son, remember that game you used to love when you were a little boy—follow the leader?"

"Yes. What about it?"

"If they're not following, Frankie, you're not leading."

The Definition of Leadership

What is leadership all about? We know it when we see it, and we certainly recognize its absence—but can we put terms to it? Can we place an intangible quality like leadership under the microscope?

Yes, we can. Jim Kouzes and Barry Posner provide this powerful definition of leadership:

> **Leadership is the art of mobilizing others to want to struggle for shared aspirations.[1]**

Let's unpack this definition to give ourselves a solid foundation for understanding true leadership.

Leadership . . .

According to *Merriam-Webster*, to *lead* is "to guide on a way," "to direct on a course or in a direction," or "to serve as a channel for." Often, leading means taking people to places they've never been before: beyond self-limiting beliefs, past obstacles, through change, and to new levels of excellence.

. . . is the art . . .

While you can analyze certain leadership behaviors, study models, and learn facts, the actual carrying out of leadership day by day is more art than science. It is a skill that improves with practice and one that can and must be applied with different styles.

. . . of mobilizing others . . .

Leadership isn't about simply maintaining the status quo. Nor is it about creating a staff of compliant employees who punch the clock and do only what they're told. Leadership mobilizes people to move forward.

. . . to want to struggle . . .

Why do people move forward? Strangely enough, it is because they want to struggle. And they want to struggle because they want the satisfaction that comes only from achieving against formidable odds.

. . . for shared aspirations.

A struggle by itself is not motivating. It is the *purpose* of the struggle that is motivating. When people have a common goal to aspire toward, it breathes life into them (fitting, given the root of the word *aspire*, which means "to breathe"). With a shared aspiration, there is nothing they will not strive to accomplish.

"For Pete's sake, I'm trying to lead, Grandma," Frank exploded. "I'm the president and CEO! But while people listen to me, I never feel like they're really hearing me!"

"Frankie, I suspect that at the moment, the janitor is more of a leader than you are. In fact, I'm sure of it, because I met him that evening you brought me by after dinner to pick up those files."

Frank stared at her. "What are you talking about?"

"The janitor is a nice man. In just the few minutes we chatted, he struck me as a trustworthy, respectful person. He was helpful and caring."

"What's your point?" asked Frank angrily.

"Leadership isn't about the nameplate on your door. It's about the character of your life."

Personal Power

Many times, businessmen and businesswomen rely on their *positional power* to lead others. Positional power relates directly to your place in the org chart and the authority that comes with it. You can have the power to fire and hire, to reward and to sanction, to command and to direct. People will, of course, respond to positional power—but if positional power is *all* you have, you will likely develop a staff of automatons. They will give only what is required of them, and not one jot more.

High-impact leadership requires something more, something beyond a nameplate on your door or a title on your business card. It requires *personal power*.

Personal power is not formally assigned to you by your organization. Personal power is granted to you by others. It is earned, based on who you are as a person. Personal power relates to your integrity, your willingness to follow through on promises, the respect you demonstrate for others, your trustworthiness, and your readiness to roll up your sleeves and go to work.

Personal power originates from within rather than from without. Therefore, it is much more potent than positional power. For example, positional power is important because it enables you to remove obstacles that stand in the way of your people. It allows you to make decisions that will streamline execution and workflow. But your personal power is what will inspire people to engage 100 percent in your business's goals and vision. When people say, "She got more out of me than I ever thought I had," or "I'd do absolutely anything for him," they are speaking of personal power.

Therefore, if you want to be a complete leader, work on your personal power. Making a difference in people's lives, influencing change, and taking your organization to the next level are all matters of character.

Frank stopped pacing and sat down heavily on the couch. "Okay, Grandma. I get your point. But I really do care about people. I want what's best for them, I do what's right, but I want what's best for my company, too. It's not wrong to want to make a profit, is it?"

"You know it's not, Frankie. When your grandfather and I ran the grocery store, we would've gone under fast if we hadn't worked hard to make a profit."

"Then what's the problem? Why do people—if I'm being honest—look at me like I'm a dictator? That's not my intention. I just want to get the job done and done well."

"Well, what do people respond to when they interact with you?"

Frank was puzzled. *"What do you mean?"*

"I mean, what do people respond to? What makes them react the way they react to you?"

"How could I possibly know?"

"You could if you put some thought into it," she said. *"People can't read your mind. They can't see into your heart. They can't peer into your soul. But they do react to what they perceive as your priorities—whether you seem more keen on taking care of their needs or only concerned with meeting goals."*

Five Leadership Styles

Robert Blake and Jane Mouton[2] pioneered a leadership model based on countless interviews they conducted. These interviews revealed that, based on observable behaviors, leaders tended to focus on two major issues: *people* and *production*. Furthermore, Blake and Mouton discovered that the varying levels of concern leaders had for these two issues defined five distinctive leadership styles, to which we've given the following names: bureaucratic, supportive, directive, traditional, or collaborative.*

The Bureaucratic Manager

We begin with the Bureaucratic Manager. These are leaders who have a *low level of concern for production*—they do only what is requested and

---

* Blake and Mouton referred to these as "managerial" styles, and that's reflected in the use of the term *manager* in the discussion below. For our purposes, we can also think of these as leadership styles.

don't go beyond the specific requirement for the results they're expected to produce. At the same time, they have a *low level of concern for people.* They become involved with people and interact with people only to the frequency and degree that are absolutely necessary. Bureaucratic Managers believe that their role is to "serve the system." They rely heavily on policies and procedures, and rarely initiate action on their own.

The director of HR in one of the companies we worked with was a classic Bureaucratic Manager. Whatever the problem, she quoted the HR manual on the subject. Period. No additions, no personal insight, no initiative. Nothing. Staff members consistently wondered why she had a job at the company, since they could read the HR manual for themselves!

However, there are times when this leadership style is not only beneficial—it is essential. For example, at a nuclear power plant where safety is the top priority, a strong compliance-oriented, by-the-book style is vital to keep processes running smoothly and to protect the public.

The Supportive Manager

The second style is the Supportive Manager. This is the leader who has a *low level of concern for production* coupled with a *high level of concern for people.* Supportive Managers firmly believe that "happy people are productive people." They believe that if they keep their people happy, productivity will just fall into place. Unfortunately, that is not always true!

This leadership style is characterized by an optimistic personality and a friendly smile. Supportive Managers want their staff to be "one big happy family." Driven by their high need for acceptance, Supportive Managers often utilize a reward system that is out of balance, over-rewarding for modest achievements.

The Supportive Manager wants harmonious relationships at all times. He or she tends to avoid conflict and displays an unwillingness to address difficult issues or to emphasize production concerns.

At Makarios Consulting, we have seen the Supportive Manager style used well and used disastrously—by the same person. We were once working with a company that was heading for possible bankruptcy. While the company had a good product, its culture was toxic, characterized by high turnover, low morale, backstabbing, and silos, all of which crippled the company's ability to function effectively.

The company hired a new president who was an off-the-chart Supportive Manager. Within a two-year period, this man completely changed the culture of the company. He walked the company through a vision and core values process, encouraged people to support one another, and broke down the silos. But he did more than that. He demonstrated personal concern for all his staff members. He didn't ask general questions such as, "How are you today?" He knew enough about his people to be specific: "How does your wife like the new minivan?" "How did your daughter's piano recital go?" "Has your son gotten over that strep throat?" His example generated goodwill and motivated people to spread it.

Unfortunately, the story doesn't end there. The company, under his leadership, pulled out of its critical dive, but then business results plateaued. The reason? His level of concern for production, as a Supportive Manager, was low. He had fixed all the people problems admirably, but he couldn't then move himself and his team to focus more intensively on business performance. Ultimately, the company let him go. There is an important lesson here: every leadership style has strengths and weaknesses. As we'll see later in this chapter, complete leaders learn to vary their leadership style to address the changing needs of their organizations over time.

The Directive Manager

In contrast to the Supportive Manager, the Directive Manager shows *high concern for production* and *low concern for people*. This style is often characterized by a "command and control" mindset. A Directive Manager may be viewed as a hard taskmaster, with abnormally high demands for output and quality and a correspondingly low tolerance for mistakes.

Directive Managers want production first, foremost, and always. They are looking for obedience. In their eyes, disagreement is equivalent to disloyalty. The Directive Manager assumes that "if you give people an inch, they'll take a mile."

Directive Managers may employ "carrot and stick" motivation. They can be generous with salary and bonuses (the carrot), but in return they expect perfection and scare people with fears about job security (the stick). Sadly, this tends to create dependent, compliant workers who don't voice their opinions freely. Their attitude says, "Just tell me what to do." They will do the minimum that is required to stay employed, and rarely identify emerging problems. In this setting, we often hear employees grouse, "If something blows up, it's not my problem."

One of our clients is a classic Directive Manager. He owns his own manufacturing company and controls all of the key decisions. He knows exactly what he wants, when he wants it, and how he wants it done. His company is modestly profitable but is not growing, and he is continually frustrated. In his words: "My people never show any initiative and creativity in addressing our customers' needs!" He regularly complains of exhaustion and work-related stress.

The truth is that, through his directive style, he has trained his people to follow orders and not think for themselves. We have coached him to engage his department heads to become more involved in key decisions affecting the company's future and to take on more day-to-day management responsibilities. We advised him that failing to do so would put the future of his business at risk because he was not developing his leaders and he had no management depth. If something happened to him, the company would fall apart. This is a typical dynamic we see with Directive Managers.

The Traditional Manager

Traditional Managers have *moderate concern for production* and *moderate concern for people*. They have a knack for compromise and for finding the middle ground. Their mantra is "I must keep things in balance."

Traditional Managers are reasonable people who are moderate in all things. Their employees see them as easy to work with and for. However, they can also be viewed as somewhat manipulative, because they are constantly assessing the politics of any situation and trying to achieve satisfaction for everyone, at every level. This habit also makes Traditional Managers very stressed!

Traditional Managers are typically very skilled at reacting to problems, putting out fires, and handling crises—while getting good, solid results from people who are relatively satisfied. All in all, this is a practical, workable leadership style. However, we consider it the second-best leadership style because of the constant battle for balance: production comes first, but only to the extent that it does not negatively affect morale.

Traditional Managers can also suffer from analysis paralysis. We saw this at a small manufacturing firm we worked with, where the head of operations needed to hire a new plant supervisor. This was a key position in the company, and a candidate had to be chosen quickly. The head of operations had reams of data on several highly qualified candidates, including leadership behavioral profiles, pre-employment surveys, and notes from no fewer than three interviews with each person.

Two months after the candidate interviews, the position remained unfilled. The head of operations was still poring over the files: looking for the ideal person, trying to find the perfect balance, seeking to make everyone above him happy. Desperate to make a fully informed, faultless decision, he could make no decision at all. During a coaching session as the process dragged on, we encouraged him to vary his leadership style—to be more directive and make a decision on the spot. He did so and chose well; the new hire flourished in the company.

The Collaborative Manager

The final leadership style is the Collaborative Manager. This style shows a *high level of concern for production* and an equally *high level of concern for people*. The Collaborative Manager's objective is to create employee satisfaction through the work itself by providing stimulating challenges to his or her people, along with the support and resources needed to meet those challenges.

There are several key places where the Collaborative Manager leadership style stands in contrast to the other four leadership styles. Leaders with any of the other styles see production needs and people needs as inherently in conflict. They therefore end up choosing one or the other, or they try to establish a static balance between the two. The Directive Manager will sacrifice his or her people's needs in order to get the job done, while the Traditional Manager will sacrifice quality or quantity if production schedules are too demanding on the staff, thereby causing a drop in morale.

Collaborative Managers, on the other hand, operate from the philosophy that organizational needs and people needs are interdependent and that there must be a *dynamic* balance between them. They understand that team members can consistently deliver superior production results only if their needs for accomplishment are being met. They believe that the best in production can only be achieved by giving the best to people. That means providing challenging work and expecting excellence, while at the same time empowering people through tools, training, support, and feedback.

Additionally, a Collaborative Manager knows that there is a difference between happiness and satisfaction. Supportive Managers seek to make their employees happy through whatever means possible. Superior production results are a separate entity entirely. The Collaborative Manager, on the other hand, doesn't focus on happiness. He or she recognizes that happiness ultimately comes from within and cannot be given to another, so instead works to foster an environment where *satisfaction* flourishes. Satisfaction comes from accomplishment. The more people accomplish, the more satisfaction they feel. Therefore, the Collaborative Manager creates a culture where achievement breeds satisfaction and where satisfaction generates further achievement in the best kind of positive feedback loop.

Finally, the Collaborative Manager is just that: collaborative. He or she proactively seeks input from employees in both planning and execution.

Collaborative leaders provide regular feedback on performance and encourage the professional development of their colleagues. They treat people's mistakes as growth opportunities for the employee and the business. In many ways, Collaborative Managers can be the toughest managers to work for: they consistently demand superior performance, and although they provide a great deal of support and resources, they also challenge you to grow, meaning that you can't be uninvested in the outcome as you might with a Directive Manager.

One of our clients is a strong Collaborative Manager. She became CEO of a manufacturing firm during a period of crisis. Her goal was not to find an acceptable balance, as a Traditional Manager would have done. It was not sufficient for things to be "good enough." Rather, she had an ultra-high concern for people and for production. She would sacrifice nothing on either side of the equation.

To pull the company out of crisis, she immediately drew in the entire leadership team and involved them in intense strategic discussions. This represented a substantial culture shift; the previous CEO had been a Directive Manager. "I may have the title of CEO, but we're *all* leaders," our client said, clearly and consistently. Her humility, her respect for others, her willingness to listen, her desire to develop others, her readiness to take on new challenges, and her passion for defining a new vision turned the company around. Within a year the company doubled its profits. More than that, the members of her leadership team openly affirmed, "I would go to hell and back for her!"

That is the power of a Collaborative Manager.

"So how do I know what people see when they look at me?" Frank asked defensively. "You say they can't read my mind—how am I supposed to read theirs to see how I come across?"

"That's easiest of all," said his grandmother calmly. "Get up, and go stand by the fireplace."

Frank frowned but obeyed out of forty years of habit. "Well?" he said, standing by the mantel and glaring at her, hands on his hips.

"Now turn around."

Frank turned. His face paled.

"Just look in the mirror, Frankie. If you take a good look, you'll see what they see."

Your Own Look in the Mirror

You may have already recognized yourself in the portraits above, or perhaps not. Be warned, though: it's easy to assume that you act in one way when in fact your behaviors show a different leadership style. Most people, when asked, say that they see themselves as either a Traditional or a Collaborative Manager. Many times, that's not an accurate self-evaluation. To help you correctly identify your dominant leadership style, we have prepared a set of questions. We encourage you to answer them with brutal honesty, then to ask two or three of your peers or advisors to answer the questions *about you* so that you can create a mini–360 degree review for yourself.

1. Which statement describes what is most important to you?

    a. We have people who are happy in their jobs and working together smoothly.

    b. We get results: on time, on budget, with the highest possible quality.

    c. We get good production while maintaining good morale.

    d. We get the best possible results with the highest level of growth from my people.

    e. We follow the appropriate processes and procedures to get the job done.

2. Which statement best describes your approach to your people?

    a. To get the results I want, I feel that it is my responsibility to give my people firm direction and manage them very closely.

    b. When it comes down to it, I won't push my people too far.

    c. I want people to come away from their job feeling like they have accomplished something of great value.

    d. People are here to do a job. They know their job description; it's up to them to fulfill it.

    e. People are at the core of our business. It's essential that we treat them well.

3. Which statement best describes your approach to production?

    a. Sometimes, in order to achieve the best results, compromise is required.

    b. If the job requires sacrifice and hard work, so be it.

    c. I believe that when I give my best to my people, they'll get the job done.

    d. I'm looking for the best, and I believe that my team has what it takes to achieve it.

    e. Growth, success, and results will flow if we follow policies and procedures.

4. When faced with a conflict between people needs and production needs, what do you tend to do?

    a. I weigh the different factors to find the middle ground.

    b. I want to retreat and not deal with it.

    c. I make sure everyone is okay first, since people who are upset can't produce.

    d. I see the conflict as an opportunity for growth for my people and for outstanding achievement.

    e. I hammer home what we need to do, how we need to do it, and when we need to have it done.

5. Typically speaking, how do you assign a task to one of your employees?

    a. I give the job to the person who wants it.

    b. I assign the task based on the person's role and responsibilities.

    c. I give the task to the person who will give me excellence, even if that requires an initial investment in growth and development.

    d. I delegate the task to the person who has the most expertise in the area.

    e. I assign the job to whoever can handle it best, given the situation.

6. Which of the following frustrates you the most often?

    a. When there's no solution that everyone will be okay with.

    b. When I can't find clear-cut guidelines or direction on how to proceed in a given circumstance.

    c. When I've done everything I can for my people, but production still isn't up to par.

    d. When no one takes initiative.

    e. When people won't give me their best.

Here's the answer key, by question. Circle the letter below based on your answers to the six questions above.

Question 1.

    a. SUPPORTIVE

    b. DIRECTIVE

    c. TRADITIONAL

    d. COLLABORATIVE

    e. BUREAUCRATIC

Question 2.

    a. DIRECTIVE

    b. TRADITIONAL

    c. COLLABORATIVE

    d. BUREAUCRATIC

    e. SUPPORTIVE

Question 3.

    a. TRADITIONAL

    b. DIRECTIVE

    c. SUPPORTIVE

    d. COLLABORATIVE

    e. BUREAUCRATIC

Question 4.

    a. TRADITIONAL

    b. BUREAUCRATIC

    c. SUPPORTIVE

    d. COLLABORATIVE

    e. DIRECTIVE

Question 5.

    a. SUPPORTIVE

    b. BUREAUCRATIC

    c. COLLABORATIVE

    d. DIRECTIVE

    e. TRADITIONAL

Question 6.

    a. TRADITIONAL

    b. BUREAUCRATIC

    c. SUPPORTIVE

    d. DIRECTIVE

    e. COLLABORATIVE

You will likely see a pattern to your answers, with the majority of them in one of the five leadership styles. This is your current dominant leadership style. Take a moment to go back a few pages and read the description of that leadership style. If you want additional information, we encourage you to take the comprehensive Styles of Leadership Survey offered by Teleometrics International.

Frank sat down again, sobered. "I do emphasize production over people, don't I, Grandma?"

"I have thought so for a long time."

"But you are what you are. I mean, people can't really change their personality, can they?"

"You don't have to, Frankie. This isn't about your personality. Your personality is just fine. This is about what you say and what you do. Change that, and everything changes."

People and Production: Finding the Balance

It was Blake and Mouton's belief that the Collaborative Manager represented the optimal leadership style and should be used almost exclusively—that is, in virtually all situations, with all people. While we don't hold with that view, as we will discuss shortly, we do believe that the collaborative style should be your "home base," philosophically and behaviorally.

The reason for this is very simple: *every leadership style except the collaborative style will provide short-term gain but long-term pain*. If you use the supportive style exclusively, your people may be happy, but production will suffer over time. The reverse occurs under the directive style: you may get things done, but at what cost to your people? The traditional leadership style will give you solid results in all things, but not the *best* results—are you satisfied with that? And the bureaucratic style appeals only to the lowest common denominator, getting done only what is necessary, with limited people development. Only by using the collaborative style as your home base will you consistently enable your people to perform at their best and deliver superior results.

The question then becomes, how do you adopt a collaborative leadership style?

Well, you must first *have clarity* about your current dominant leadership style. As we indicated previously, be thorough and honest in your self-evaluation, and seek the evaluation and input of others. You may not like what you find. That's all right! This is your opportunity for positive change.

Next, *get specific*. It is impossible to come into the office one morning and say, "Today I am going to become a collaborative leader!" Instead, pick a project in which you're going to lead a team, and pilot a collaborative leadership behavior in that setting. Don't be vague. Write down exactly what you are going to do differently and what you hope it will accomplish. This is key! For reference, here are some of the commitments that make up the collaborative leadership style. You can draw upon these ideas to design more specific tasks and goals for yourself:

- I will maximize the involvement of my team members in the planning, goal-setting, and execution phases of this project.

- I will encourage and reward creativity and initiative from my team members.

- I will make resources (i.e., training, funds, and personnel) available to my team to support them in their efforts.

- I will integrate myself as an active team member when appropriate.

- I will encourage my team members to draw upon their special knowledge and skills.

- I will look out for tasks that present developmental opportunities for team members and assign these tasks to ensure their professional growth.

- I will provide regular performance feedback to my team.

By writing down what you are going to do, how you are going to do it, and the results you are driving for, you open the door to accountability.

Your list will help you take the next step toward adopting a collaborative style and *hold yourself accountable.* But don't stop there. Engage the team you are leading. Inform them that you are trying to improve your leadership style, and tell them what you intend to do differently. Tell them what deliverables you are hoping to achieve not only on the production side of things but also on the people side. Request that they let you know if you are slipping into old patterns of behavior.

Finally, once the project is completed, spend some time in *reflection and evaluation.* Don't expect that you will have done everything right the first time. Chances are, circumstances arose during the course of the project in which you were "all thumbs" or you fell back into your dominant leadership style. What you're seeking here is to establish a new trend and direction, and to become comfortable with a new home base.

Be sure to analyze both production and people results carefully. Did you produce what you needed to produce? Were your people empowered to accomplish the project? Did they feel satisfied at its conclusion?

With one project under your belt, select the next project to work on from a collaborative leadership standpoint. Practice again and again until the style becomes natural and familiar to you. Don't worry that in the beginning the style doesn't feel comfortable. This is a case where doing precedes feeling. When you see the results for both people and production, you will begin to believe in the process of collaborative leadership— and in yourself as a collaborative leader!

"Let me see if I understand this, Grandma," said Frank, sitting down and leaning forward earnestly. "If I want to be a better leader—a complete leader—I need to increase my concern for my people without sacrificing the quality of my production. Right?"

"Well said, dear."

"We have this big project on a tight timeline coming up. We're developing very complex software to drive a new communications system for a client. Now, normally, I would bring everyone together, give them their marching orders, watch them closely, and hound them nonstop. That may get the job done, but it's going to kill morale, isn't it?"

"I certainly wouldn't enjoy working under those conditions, Frankie."

Frank winced but went on doggedly: "So to change, I need to do things like ask questions—real questions that generate real feedback—from my people, and encourage their creativity and innovation."

"That is an excellent place to start," his grandmother said with approval.

"Then I'll need to delegate more—assign leads for the various aspects of the project and let them do their job. You know," he said in surprise, "that would really free up my time for some larger strategic decisions."

His grandmother smiled. "See, Frankie, once you acknowledge the problem, it's fairly easy to figure out the elements of a solution."

Frank grimaced, still following the thread of his own thought, and said, "And I suppose I'll have to give people more feedback and support."

"It probably won't come naturally at first, Frankie—but the proof is in the pudding. I think you'll find plenty of proof."

Frank sat back and thought about it. "You know, I think I will. But I'm bothered by something—aren't there times when you have to really crack the whip?"

"There is a time and a season for all things," his grandmother said with a smile. "That is a principle that has been around for rather a long time, one that your grandfather and I had to learn pretty quickly in our business. But to answer your question more specifically, yes. Life is a series of unique people and unique situations. One rule never fits all."

Tailoring Style to Situation

The people you lead are individuals. Some will respond best to one approach, some to another. Also, various situations will call for different leadership styles. For example, you will—and should—act differently in an emergency customer situation than at a strategic planning retreat. Therefore, you need to be able to vary your style yet always come back to your collaborative home base.

So how do you know which style to use in which situation? You need to become a detective, constantly analyzing and evaluating what's going on around you. Here are some important clues to watch out for.

Stay *collaborative* when you see

- the need to build and maintain open communication;
- the importance of identifying and drawing upon the resources, ideas, and creativity of the group;
- a need to facilitate the learning and development of group members; or
- the necessity of active support, commitment, and follow-up by members.

Become *supportive* when you find that

- temporary relaxation is required so that group members can reduce tensions built up over a stressful work period;
- others have a strong desire to have their own way on a situation or approach which has minimal business impact;
- team members are very tense or overly emotional about the situation they face; or
- pleasant and harmonious feelings among members are more important than accomplishing tasks in the near term.

Move to the *directive* if you discover that

- your team members really do have to be told what to do because they lack training or are frightened;

- you and you alone have the knowledge, experience, and expertise relevant to the issue or task at hand;

- there is a real emergency, and no time is available for checking with others;

- the feelings, support, and commitment of others are less critical than near-term results; or

- the solution is non-negotiable (safety concerns, legal constraints, etc.).

Seek the balance of being *traditional* if

- political considerations require compromise;

- you are concerned with overburdening a team member who has too much on his or her plate;

- it is important to recognize differences of opinion without actually exploring the basis of the differences;

- it is important to get the best possible results with limited resources available to you; or

- you are trying to satisfy a Directive Manager while at the same time meeting your employees' needs.

Shift to the *bureaucratic* when

- a routine operating procedure has been established and accepted by those involved and has proven effective; or

- you really have nothing to contribute and are not impacted by the outcome of a particular issue or situation.

You might have been surprised to see that there are times to become more bureaucratic in your leadership style, but there truly are. Take this example. A VP was once explaining a project to one of his staff in a very collaborative mode. But the woman stopped him and said, "I don't know how to do this, and I'm scared. Just tell me what you want done. I don't need lots of dialogue, and I don't need to be involved in the decision-making process. I won't be bruised—I promise! Just tell me what you want done and I'll go do it." The VP was surprised but said, "Oh, okay! Go do these three things." She thanked him, went and did them, and the project continued smoothly.

"So being an effective leader means I need to be constantly aware, constantly on the alert . . . and constantly flexible to meet the needs of my people and the situation. I'm not gonna lie—that seems overwhelming!"

"It's work, Frankie, but it's not impossible. Like Nike says, 'Just do it!'"

6 Simple Steps for Varying Your Style

Varying your style doesn't have to be overwhelming. It is simply a matter of following these six straightforward steps:

1. **Don't ignore the signs until you suddenly have a fire on your hands.** Pay attention to clues—like the ones listed above—to evaluate your production needs and your people needs. Let your analysis cover the general (the project, the team, the company) as well as the specific (this person, this task, this problem).

2. **Acknowledge that it's time to shift your style.** Accept your evaluation and your analysis, then make your decision as to what style you need to shift to. Don't wait. Take action!

3. **Write down what you are going to do.** Sound familiar? Just as you wrote down your action plan for shifting to collaborative home base, you can do the same when you need to shift to any other mode. Writing down what you intend and what you hope to accomplish slows you down, gives you specific tasks and behaviors to engage in, and allows you to measure your success. It also prevents you from going to the opposite extreme in a pendulum swing. For instance, if you realize that directive behavior is called for, writing

down that you will do specific tasks X, Y, and Z will allow you to engage in those tasks and then return to your collaborative home base position promptly—rather than continue on in the directive style until you go overboard and become autocratic.

Remember that when you write out what you are going to do, you should include what you are going to do with regard to people as well as to production. Leaders tend to recognize what they need to do to increase production: they engage in *directive behaviors*, such as defining roles, setting goals, organizing work, controlling processes, establishing timelines, and directing activities. It is less intuitive to identify what needs to be done to meet people needs. People needs are best met by drawing upon *supportive behaviors* like active listening, two-way communication, open discussions, verbal support, regular feedback, and mutual problem solving.

4. **Keep your actions and words business focused.** Everything you do—both for people and for production—should be focused on business. Your ultimate goal is to get the job done and produce superior business results. For example, you may realize that an employee is floundering due to stress and that you should shift to a supportive approach. Prepare two or three pertinent questions, pose them to the employee, and let them share their thoughts and feelings. Once the person has done so and you have heard their concerns, you can then discuss how to proceed to solve the business problem.

5. **Examine the results of varying your style.** There are three questions you should ask yourself when evaluating your efforts to vary your style:

    - Did I choose the right style?

    - Did I execute effectively?

    - Did I get the results I was looking for?

    If you didn't get the results you were looking for, you could have had the right style but not implemented it well, or you could have decided on the wrong style to start with. Ultimately, you'll know whether you chose your style correctly and adopted it effectively because you'll get positive results when you do. Those results should be twofold: you got the job done and done well, and your people are satisfied and engaged. You will know the former by looking at the facts. You will know the latter by asking for feedback.

6. **Return to your collaborative home base.** Varying your leadership style is temporary; do so to meet an immediate, short-term need. To *consistently* meet both people and production needs at the highest possible level and with the highest possible return, go back to your collaborative home-base position and lead from that style the majority of the time.

 ══

"I can do this, can't I?" asked Frank slowly.

His grandmother smiled. "Of course you can. Leadership is a skill, and a skill can be learned. You want to, so you will. It is as simple as that."

ZEROING IN: *STRATEGY*

Frank saw the last guest out and closed the door. His grandmother's dining room table sat twelve, and every Sunday evening she had a full house. Her meals were legendary. After all, he thought to himself with a smile, she had been around long enough to become a legend!

He walked back to the dining room, collected the last of the coffee cups, and brought them into the kitchen to join the formidable stacks of dishes, bowls, cutlery, and pans on the counter. His grandmother looked at the pile somewhat ruefully. "I admit, this is my least favorite part," she said. "But it doesn't get smaller by staring at it!"

"Would you like me to wash or dry?" asked Frank encouragingly.

"Wash, thank you. Then I can dry them and put them away immediately."

Frank turned on the taps and waited for the water to heat up. "I really don't know how you do it," he said. "People positively vie for the privilege of coming here to eat. Your menus are so varied and delicious! How do you keep it up every week?"

His grandmother smiled. "I know exactly what I want to accomplish, Frankie. And I stay focused on that goal. I don't let anything—whether the lure of convenience foods or the temptations of gourmet magazines—distract me from doing what I do best."

Strategy Matters

Successful businesses quickly learn that they must establish a realistic set of goals that will guide them as they grow, and then develop a strategy to achieve those goals that will work effectively in the face of stiff competition. From that will flow the effective allocation of resources that will enable the business to achieve sustained competitive advantage.

Let's start with a definition of *strategy*. Michael Porter, professor at Harvard Business School, teaches that strategy is something that "explains how an organization, faced with competition, will achieve superior performance."[3]

An effective strategy, executed well, can enable you to deliver better results than your competitors because it can help you define a unique position in the marketplace. It helps you answer two key questions: "What value will your organization create?" and "How will you capture some of that value for yourself?"[4]

A solid business strategy is vital to the complete leader. It enables you to achieve superior performance in your business by creating unique value for your customers, keeping you focused on your target market, and making it easier to identify the right business opportunities to deliver sustainable growth. Now, let's discover how to get there.

"You stay focused on your goal," mused Frank. "I wonder . . ."

"You wonder what?" asked his grandmother neutrally.

Frank shrugged. "Just thinking about focus. About goals and vision. I thought we shared the same vision among the leadership team at my company, but lately I haven't been so sure."

"Well, how would you define your vision?"

"Simple." Frank grinned, dunked a plate in sudsy water, and began to scrub. "To sell our products, sweep the market, and become a huge success story! Isn't that everyone's vision?"

"Yes, Frankie—that is everyone's vision. And that's why so few reach it, I expect. It's pie-in-the-sky. It has no meat to it. What does it mean? What does it look like?"

Frank handed her the dripping plate, puzzled. "So how would you define a vision?"

His grandmother looked thoughtfully at the dirty dishes. "Take this meal. All my meals. I suppose you could say they are the product of my vision—a vision I formed after your grandfather died eighteen years ago. I knew that if I didn't take positive steps, I would end up a lonely, bitter old woman. So I decided to become a very specialized hostess. I gave myself a year to build up speed, but my goal was there from the outset: to invite people over every week and give them an enjoyable evening centered around a memorable meal. But I knew my limitations, so I wanted that meal to taste gourmet without the time it takes to cook gourmet."

"And how is that more practical than my vision for my company?"

"With this in mind, I have never concerned myself with extras—music, flower arrangements, entertainment, games, and whatnot. I just focus on the food. And I don't go crazy with the food: it has to be easy to prepare. But the final taste test has to make my guests ask me for the recipe! So my vision gave me a time frame, boundaries, and direction. It made sure, and still makes sure, that I get where I want to go."

Establish the Vision

Establishing your vision is the first step in creating a working strategy for your company. Vision is the inspirational engine that drives strategy. Vision is where we begin.

One of the problems we face in business is that the word *vision* has connotations of amorphousness or outrageousness. Visions can be so vague that they are useless in the day-to-day running of the business, or so ridiculous in scope that everybody knows they are impossible. Either way, such a vision is not worth the paper it is printed on or the breath used to recite it.

Your vision for your company should be a *realistic statement of aspiration* based on what you are today and what you want to become in the future. It should be practical, specific, and targeted to help you generate the most value possible from the enterprise you are running. There should be a time frame around it to identify long-term and short-term goals, strategies, and tactics. And finally, the vision should be measurable so you will know if you are making progress toward achieving it.

Bad Vision: To be the biggest automotive parts company in the world!

This statement is too vague ("biggest in the world"). What is your definition of "biggest"? Is it sales? Number of employees? Number of locations? By when should this happen? And how does any of that contribute to bringing unique value to your customers?

Good Vision: To be the highest revenue provider of engines and drive trains for the high-performance automotive market in the United States within ten years.

This statement is practical and specific, and provides focus within a specific time frame. It is long term but can be measured.

To establish an engaging vision for your company, follow this five-step process:

1. **Stop and Listen.** Vision starts by stopping. Stop and take the time to think through what your customers are conveying to you about your business and the value they crave, what is happening in the marketplace around you, and what your employees are telling you. Then you need to listen to people, consider what they are saying, and weigh the value of their input objectively—all of which takes real humility. Demonstrate your belief that people have something worth saying and insights worth using. As you listen, drop any pride or ego that may crop up.

2. **Discuss.** Take your leadership team through a series of structured conversations focused on questions such as these:

    *   What is our mission? Why is our company in business—what difference do we make?

- What business do we want to be in ten years from now? What is our measurable ten-year target?

- What are our core values—the behaviors that will ensure our success?

Put all the ideas on the table without trying to evaluate or word-smith anything. Just talk it through—thoroughly.

3. **Cull.** Once all the ideas are out in the open, engage in a culling process. Some ideas will be thrown out—not necessarily because they are bad, but because they are not applicable or workable at this time. Others will be kept just as they are. Some ideas can be combined into a single overarching thought. This process will show you what themes really stand out: this is the basis for your vision.

4. **Refine.** Now that you've filtered raw ideas into a few themes, refine the themes. Ask yourself, "What does this mean? What does it look like? How will we measure if we are achieving it?" Seek to verbalize your vision, remembering that your vision will guide your thoughts and decisions from here on out. So keep it tight! You don't want a twenty-five-watt bulb; you want a laser beam.

5. **Test.** Finally, test your vision by asking for feedback on it from the top down. Make sure it is a vision that can be shared by everyone in the company, from the members of the leadership team to every individual in the rank and file. Properly developed, your vision will become a unifying force for your company as you move forward. The goal is to have every member of your team understand your vision and be willing to support it.

Establishing a strategic vision truly does make a concrete difference. A small manufacturing company we worked with had not taken the time to establish its vision and was muddling along with no growth or sense of direction. With our guidance, the CEO and her team took the time to define the vision in practical, measurable terms and then to present it to the entire employee base. The vision was to double the company's revenue and earnings in three years, and grow their share of the precision-medical products market in which they compete by 30 percent. Developing the vision became a galvanizing event, making it much easier for the leadership team to define a set of measurable strategic goals and to execute effectively on a daily basis. The result was a dramatic turnaround in profitability in two years, all tied to the vision they had adopted.

"We're sure not getting where we want to go," admitted Frank. "Perhaps if I spent more time hammering out a better vision with my leadership team, we could get some forward momentum going."

"That may not be enough," his grandmother said quietly.

He handed her a dripping serving platter. "What do you mean?"

"Well, a moment ago I said that I knew my limitations. I'm not a gourmet cook. Never have been; never will be."

"So?"

"To be blunt, Frankie, I suspect that you have an inflated vision of yourself and your company. And ironically enough, until you pop that balloon, it's only going to weigh you down."

Assess Your Current Position

Vision defines where you want the business to go. Assessment of your company confirms where you are today. These two points work hand in hand to define the gap you have to cross—the gap your strategy will bridge.

Your assessment should include the following:

- **The numbers:** What do your financial statements and the numbers related to your customer base, retention, conversions, and so on tell you?

- **The products:** How do your products or services eliminate your prospects' and customers' pain?

- **The processes:** How would you evaluate the efficiency, cost-effectiveness, and consistency of your organizational processes?

- **The market:** What is happening in the marketplace that affects your business?

- **The customer:** What is the profile of your current customers, including demographics, technographics, and psychographics?

- **The buzz:** What is your reputation? What are you hearing from your customer service department, your sales team, and social media?

- **The issues:** What business issues are inhibiting your growth, whether internal or external in nature?

- **The leadership:** How well does your leadership team work together, solve problems, and hold individual members accountable?

The most critical aspect of assessing your company is the ability to be brutally honest. It is human nature to avoid facing our weaknesses. But the fact is, a true assessment of your company will likely reveal some warts.

For that reason, you have to be objective and willing to go where the facts take you. Don't slip into the trap of assuming, "Everyone wants what we've got!" or of letting your pride claim, "We've never been stronger!" Always come back to "What do we actually *know*?"

This is going to take time. Probably serious time; often this can take weeks. It is not a half-hour discussion based on people's impressions of where you are. A careful assessment will demand that you dig deep for information, analyze it and cross-check it, and extrapolate from it a true profile of your company.

"You do have a way of cutting to the chase, don't you, Grandma?" asked Frank without rancor.

"I'm just being practical, dear."

"And I bet I know where you're going next. We have to assess the competition, too."

"You can never dismiss your competition out of hand," agreed his grandmother. *"Just saying they're nothing won't make them go away. Even I have competition, you know."*

"You?" Frank said in surprise.

"Of course. I'm competing against the lure of the sports games that are on TV this evening, against the convenience of pizza being delivered to the front door, and against the sheer weariness of needing to get up and go to work tomorrow. I know that. So I offer my guests something better."

Frank looked at her with a sudden smile. *"That you do, Grandma, that you do!"*

Analyze the Competition

Analyzing your competition needs to be part of your strategic planning process—and part of your daily business life. Your business doesn't exist in a vacuum. You are part of a dynamic market that is surging with competitors.

Some companies are your direct competitors: they sell the exact products or services that you do to the very same customers. Other companies offer indirect competition: they nibble at the edges of your target market, offering similar-but-different products or services, claiming business you might otherwise garner for yourself.

To thoroughly analyze your competition, avail yourself of all the information you can lay your hands on. That includes annual reports, financial statements, marketing campaigns, employee profiles, third-party reports, and news items. And don't forget to talk to people. Talk to your own customers to determine why they chose you over the competition. Talk to former customers who have left you for the competition. Talk to vendors who may have insights into your competition.

Once you have all this data, categorize your competitors by product, service, location, size, reputation, price, and any other key metrics. You want to know where you are different and where you are the same. Seek to put yourself in the mind of your prospects and customers. Where is their pain? What drives their decision-making process? You need to be able to view your competitors dispassionately and see what makes them attractive to prospects. Talk to their customers. Read the reviews their clients post online. Make inquiries at trade shows and networking events.

By gaining a clear understanding of the competitive landscape in which you do business, you will deepen your understanding of the unique value you must create. You will be able to close the gap between where you are today and where you want to be. You may unearth new, untapped markets. You may discover ways to modify your products or services to satisfy more customers than ever before. You may identify a new brand or message that will transform your presence in the marketplace.

In every case, one thing is certain: an objective analysis will make you much smarter about your own business and increase your chances of creating unique value in the marketplace. With that in mind, you are more likely to outperform your competitors and get and keep the customers you want.

Frank became thoughtful as he began working on the cutlery. "How would you describe yourself, Grandma? I mean, can you put into words what makes you better than all those alternatives?"

"I suppose I would say it's 'simple food with a flair' coupled with 'easy to make on your own,'" his grandmother replied. "I don't cook ethnic, because a lot of the people I know don't care for it. So I only use common ingredients—chicken, beef, carrots, corn, whatever—but I give them a rich flavor by the herbs, spices, and sauces I make. Everyone who comes to my table knows that if they like what I serve, I'll give them the recipe and it won't be too hard to re-create at home."

"'Simple food with a flair' and 'easy to make on your own,'" repeated

Frank. "It's amazing that those two down-to-earth guidelines yield such out-of-this-world meals!"

"What sets you apart doesn't have to be complicated, Frankie. Just compelling."

Define Your Differentiators

Defining your differentiators is truly the crux of creating an effective strategy for your business. Your differentiators enable you to build a compelling case for prospective customers to choose you over other firms and to stay with you. Communicating what sets you apart in clear, memorable terms makes it easy for prospects to understand why you are the right choice.

To define your differentiators, it's important to understand that *your* unique position in the marketplace is not determined by one thing alone. Rather, your differentiating qualities and capabilities are the result of a combination of factors. These factors, when combined, create a powerful position for your firm. For example, at Makarios Consulting, we differentiate ourselves by combining

- a unique approach that helps businesses shape their strategy, execute it, and build healthy leadership teams to sustain their growth;
- a robust and proprietary leadership development program;
- personal experience in business, which gives us wisdom we can share; and
- a personal touch that strengthens our ability to serve as trusted advisors.

Do other consulting firms offer one or more of these differentiators? Yes, but few offer our combination. And it's that combination that sets us apart. When considering your differentiators, the whole is truly greater than the sum of its parts.

Furthermore, *the individual components that differentiate you do not have to be complicated.* Too often, leadership teams waste a good deal of time trying to come up with a differentiator that they believe is new, innovative, or unheard of in the marketplace. That is almost always impossible, since there is little new under the sun.

Differentiators are usually, in and of themselves, quite simple. Consider one of the companies we worked with: a small heating and air conditioning company. The president claimed that one of his key differentiators (among several) was that his company answered the phone when you called. No answering service, no menu, no voicemail. Period.

In fact, we could be in the middle of a coaching session with him, and if a phone rang more than three times he would break off the conversation and answer the phone himself. He swore that it was this unfailing level of customer service that put him ahead of his competitors.

As you define your differentiators, remember too that *customers buy for very specific reasons*. The ultimate purpose of your differentiators is to help you get and keep customers. For that reason, you need to have a deep and precise understanding of why your customers are buying from you and why your competitors' customers are buying from them.

This analysis requires both clarity and emotional separation. For your own customers, you may need to let go of preconceived notions as to why people buy from you. For instance, a manufacturing firm selling electronic sensors to the military had assumed that their customers were buying because of the way their sales and service team made the sale and followed up afterward. The firm's leadership discovered later that the real differentiator was that the parts were made in the United States and could be shipped for next-day delivery. The attention of the sales team made some difference, but it was not essential. US-based manufacturing and guaranteed delivery time were critical.

It is essential to define your differentiators with clarity. Doing so will help you define where you invest time, money, technology, and personnel—and those definitions can make or break your business. Compare these two situations:

- The board of a private golf club determined that it could differentiate its club through a combination of excellent service and the superior condition of the course. The staff had previously cut corners on cost (i.e., coarse sand for the sand traps and an understaffed dining room) and sacrificed excellence. When the board saw other clubs in the area cutting corners, it made the strategic decision to invest in more staffing, higher-quality service, and improvements to the grounds. Membership grew in response.

- A private nine-hole golf course assumed that its members wanted a "country club experience." Therefore, the board added a fancy dining pavilion and expensive golf carts, raising dues to cover those expenses. Membership declined. Members later shared that they had actually enjoyed the relaxed, informal feeling of the club along with its low cost. The board misunderstood what its members were buying and chose the wrong differentiators.

Defining your differentiators enhances your unique position in the marketplace, raising a barrier against your competition and allowing you to capture your highest growth opportunities at the greatest margin.

"I have to think about what really differentiates us from our competition," Frank said, his gaze growing unfocused. "I think we've let ourselves get slack. We got a little proud, and that led to getting a little lazy."

"That can happen all too easily," agreed his grandmother. "And the best way to avoid it is to have a plan to keep you on track and to constantly ask what it is that makes you different. Just like I make sure to ask my guests what really made the evening fun for them."

Develop a Specific Plan with Measurable Goals

Once you know what your vision is, understand where your company is today, and appreciate the competitive environment and what differentiates you, you can then establish a specific plan with measurable goals to close the gap between where you are and where you want to be.

Creating this plan takes strategy out of the realm of theory and into the arena of practicality. Your plan should establish your strategic goals for whatever time period is relevant for your business and market: typically three to five years.

First, agree on the general areas where you want to focus your resources. This helps get the leadership team on the same page. Companies commonly establish goals in areas such as these:

- New customer acquisition / sales growth

- Cost management / margin improvement

- Leadership development

- Marketing / sales activity

Once you have agreed upon the general goal areas, it's time to define SMART goals—that is, goals that are Specific, Measurable, Achievable, Relevant, and Timely:

- **Specific.** A good goal has to answer certain questions, including:
  - How much?
  - In what time frame?
  - To what end?

- **Measurable.** Your goal should be written in such a way that the metric itself is obvious (number of customers, conversion ratio, cost savings, etc.) and can be tracked weekly, monthly, quarterly, and annually to ensure that your plan is successful.

- **Achievable.** The best goals are a stretch. They demand that everyone work hard to help the organization grow. Therefore, a good goal is usually something that is beyond your current reach—without being an overreach. The goal needs to remain achievable.

- **Relevant.** Your goals need to remain relevant to your overarching vision. Some goals may be good in and of themselves but will not further your business strategy. Regardless of their intrinsic worth, they must be discarded in favor of goals that are relevant to the needs of your business.

- **Timely.** A strategic goal without a time frame is a fantasy. Without a time frame, you will not have a sense of urgency, and you will not have the ability to measure how you are progressing. A deadline makes the goal a concrete commitment and helps you manage yourself and your teams accordingly.

Consider two examples—one of a tangible goal (membership) and one of an intangible goal (reputation):

Bad Goal: Grow our membership.
- By how much?
- By when?
- Targeting what kind of people?

Good Goal: Increase our proprietary members from 280 to 320 with an additional waiting list of 20 by January 1, 2014.
- Specific: defines the target as proprietary members.
- Measurable: defines success as going from 280 to 320 people, plus a waiting list of 20.
- Achievable: represents a significant but attainable growth rate.
- Relevant: business health depends on membership growth.
- Timely: sets a deadline.

Bad Goal: Improve the reputation of the company.
- What does "reputation" mean?
- How will this be measured?
- Where is the time frame?

Good Goal: To increase the company's Net Promoter® score[5] by 10 points by July 2014.
- Specific: addresses one specific aspect of reputation, namely the Net Promoter score, which measures the loyalty that exists between a

provider and a consumer. It is based on a direct question: "How likely are you to recommend our company/product/service to your friends?"

- Measurable: defines the metric in terms of Net Promoter points.

- Achievable: represents a significant but achievable level of improvement.

- Relevant: business depends on generating positive customer experiences.

- Timely: sets a deadline.

By developing your plan around SMART goals, you squeeze the ambiguity out of what you want to accomplish. You give your vision and your strategy a specific form. This sets you up to design actionable tactics to accomplish those goals.

You also give yourself the gift of confidence. A good strategy and a set of SMART goals helps you see exactly where you are going. And if you can see it, you can achieve it!

———

One final and important point: in our experience, there are many circumstances that can derail strategy. Here are three we see often:

Strategy gets derailed when you compete to be "the best."[6] Competing to be the best is not nearly as effective as aiming to be unique. "The best" is a difficult place to define and attain. But "unique" is both concrete and achievable. Your goal should be to create unique value for your customers— to deliver something your competitors cannot. What *differentiates* you from your competitors is what will enable you to sustain success.

Strategy gets derailed when you try to please everyone. Your objective in business is *not* to make every customer happy. Your objective is to decide which customers you want to make happy and how to do that most effectively. And then, wow them! Accept the fact that there will be a set of customers who will be in some fashion dissatisfied, and learn to live with it. Otherwise, your customers—not your strategy—will determine the deployment of your resources.

Strategy gets derailed when you can't say no. There are many opportunities in the business world. Some will complement your business strategy and others won't. Some may fit your goals in theory but would stretch your resources too thin. It is easy to say, "That's a great idea! Let's do it!" But if the idea, no matter how great it is, dilutes your purpose, prevents you from accomplishing your growth goals, or inhibits you from taking on opportunities that would help you achieve those goals, then you should put it aside. You have to be able to give a meaningful no before you can offer a meaningful yes.

Frank handed the last dish to his grandmother for drying and wiped his hands on a fresh towel. "You know what I think, Grandma?"

"What's that, dear?"

He grinned. "I think we can really cook up something special at our company if we all put our heads together!"

His grandmother's eyes twinkled. "I've never doubted it, Frankie!"

SLOWING DOWN AND LISTENING UP:
COMMUNICATION

"Frankie. Frankie!"

Frank's grandmother's voice impinged on his thoughts. He jerked his head up guiltily. "Yes, Grandma?"

She skewered him with a glance. "You haven't heard a word I've said, have you?"

"Of course I have!" Frank protested. But he felt the flush rising.

"Then what did I just ask you?"

"Well . . . um . . ."

The 6 Obstacles to Effective Communication

The most important skill of any leader is the ability to communicate effectively. If a leader cannot clearly articulate his or her vision, cannot connect with people in such a way as to promote understanding, or cannot listen so as to really hear what people have to say, then he or she will never become a complete leader.

So what stops us from effectively articulating, connecting, understanding, and listening?

We're moving too fast. We cannot ignore the impact of the world we live in. Technology today has increased the speed of business astronomically. Sadly, communication often suffers as a result.

Because technology allows us to communicate instantaneously, we tend to fall into the trap of communicating with no thought, no consideration, and no attention to what we say or how we say it. Pick up the phone and make the call. Type the email and hit send. Text. IM. Tweet. Words flow fast and furious, but they are not the right words, given in the right way, capable of achieving the right end.

We're listening too little. People have never been very good at listening, and technology and the speed of business only make things worse. Poor listening can occur for a variety of reasons. For instance, we may not be listening attentively because

- we are facing a personal or work problem that is diverting our attention;
- we don't care about what is being said;
- we disagree with what is being said;
- we've never learned active listening skills; or
- we are distracted by multiple tasks (checking email while talking, surfing the web, reading a report, etc.).

We're failing to show respect. We tend to forget that people have always had—and always will have—the need to be heard. This isn't about sound waves traveling through the air. People want to be treated with courtesy and respect. They want to know that the person they are speaking with is 100 percent present with them.

There was one instance when we were leaving one of our client firms and met one of the corporate executives in the stairwell. We greeted him, and he began to ask a few questions while pounding down the stairs. As he asked his last question, he went out the door. The door actually shut *before we had the chance to answer him*. He never stopped. He never looked back. And the questions he was asking were important to the business! We wondered, "Is this the way he 'listens' to his people?"

If you attempt to communicate but don't demonstrate respect or give the other person your full attention, the process will be self-defeating—destructive to the other person and to the relationship between the two of you.

We're making assumptions. An assumption is something that we accept as true without proof. Miscommunication happens when we make assumptions regarding the following:

- *Definitions.* Words are our most basic units of communication. They can trip us up, though, when a term is defined differently by the speaker and the listener, is loaded with additional meaning because of an individual's personal experience, or isn't properly understood because the listener has an area of ignorance.

- *Content.* When one party assumes that they know what the other party is going to say, they mentally tune out.

- *Expectations.* If I assume I know what you expect of me, I will act on that assumption rather than listen to what you are actually asking or telling me.

We're ignoring the importance of nonverbal communication. Communication isn't only about words. Your entire body is involved in communication. That includes your body language, such as crossed arms (a "well-defended" gesture that is usually experienced by others as being unfriendly); facial expressions, such as rolled eyes, frowns, and smirks; and nonverbal vocalizations, such as sighs. Consider the power of nonverbal communication in the following example:

> You are walking down the corridor at work and the CEO is walking the opposite direction. As the two of you approach each other, you say to the CEO, "Can I see you for a couple of minutes?"
>
> The CEO, in a very welcoming, positive tone says, "Sure, why not?" and at the same time looks at his watch.

What is your assessment of the CEO's actual willingness to talk with you right then? You probably decide that "now isn't the best time." Why?

Because there is a conflict between the verbal message and the nonverbal message. The CEO's words said yes, but his actions said no. When there is a conflict between the verbal message and the nonverbal message, we tend to believe what we see, not what we hear. That is, we believe the nonverbal more than the verbal.

We're not checking for understanding. Just because you've spoken—and even spoken carefully—doesn't mean you have communicated. Communication requires understanding. Unfortunately, we usually fail to verify that the message really landed or check whether the facts are actually clear in the other person's mind.

Many business leaders protest, "I don't have time to check for understanding!" But the truth of the matter is, you are going to spend more time on the back end dealing with the mess that results from miscommunication than you will ever spend by taking a few minutes on the front end checking for understanding.

Frank's grandmother folded her hands in her lap. "Now then, Frankie. Suppose you tell me what's on your mind?"

"What do you mean?"

"You're preoccupied. What happened today?"

Frank sighed. "Oh, I'm just frustrated, I guess. We had this big kick-off meeting for a new project two weeks ago. I've been trying to back off my people a bit and let them do their jobs without watching over their shoulders. Well, we had our first status meeting on it today, and I find out that two of my leaders—two really good people!—hadn't done anything on the project." He frowned. "That's not accurate. One hadn't done anything. The other had gone off in a complete wrong direction."

"How did they explain what they did?"

"The first claimed she didn't know that a certain deliverable was hers! Impossible! And the other honestly thought he had done what was needed. He explained his rationale to me afterward. I could swear he was

in a different kickoff meeting! I don't know where the miscommunication happened!"

"Well, Frankie, I suspect it happened with you."

Frank reared his head back. "What?"

His grandmother was calm. "You just said the two are really good people. So they weren't lazy, and they weren't stupid. The direction in the meeting came from you. You had the primary responsibility to make sure they understood what was required of them. You obviously didn't."

"I asked everyone if they had any questions!" protested Frank.

"Yes," said his grandmother, "but how did you ask?"

Asking the Right Questions, at the Right Time

Many of us believe that if we ask lots of questions as a way to engage the other person, then we are therefore communicating well and connecting with the other person. This may or may not be the case. We must ask the *right* questions at the *right* time to get the information we need in order to truly communicate effectively.

When used properly, questions

- provide us with information we might not otherwise have gained;

- permit us to control the flow and amount of communication; and

- show that we have interest in the other person's thoughts, feelings, and ideas.

And yet, most leaders have no idea how to use questions—what kind, when to use them, and when not to use them.

There are two different kinds of questions we can ask another person: open and closed.

Closed questions

Most of the questions we ask each other are closed questions, meaning they can be answered with yes or no. Unfortunately, a closed question rarely gives us actionable information. This means that when we are asking closed questions, we often are not getting useful information in return.

Closed questions can begin with any number of words, such as *can*, *will*, *do*, *should*, *are*, and *could*. But no matter how they begin, they generally allow only for a monosyllabic response. The lure of closed questions is that they seem efficient: we ask a question, we get a one-word answer, we go on about our business. The trap of closed questions is that they too often do not tell us everything we need to know.

For instance, suppose you ask the question, "Do you understand?" Typically, people will automatically say yes—even if they don't have a clue what is going on. Why? Because they are afraid that if they say no, they will appear stupid, and they know that a yes is what the person wants. Therefore, that particular closed question usually not only fails to aid the situation but actually derails positive action. Every military officer knows that when the commanding officer concludes his orders with "Any questions," the desired response is "No, sir!" A better question to ask is, "*What* questions do you have?" This sounds more like a genuine invitation for members of the group to discuss, question, contribute, and debate, and is an example of an *open question*.

Open questions

Conversely, while we ask open questions much more infrequently, we get valuable information in return much more often. This information is something concrete, something we can rely on, something we can work with.

There are only six different words that can begin an open question: *who*, *what*, *when*, *where*, *why*, and *how*. You could also add two additional expressions that help draw out information: "Tell me more!" and "Because . . . ?"

The key here is that open questions require more than a single-word response. They ask for information (rather than simple assent or dissent): data, details, demonstration of comprehension, etc.

To better understand the difference between open and closed questions and where each brings value to business communication, let's look at how journalists and physicians gather data.

Journalists: Open-Question Experts

Journalists write news stories using a formula: the first paragraph of the story (called the "lead"), which is usually no more than two sentences, answers all six open questions: who, what, when, where, why, and how. The rest of the story is an elaboration of the data in the first paragraph. Because they need all the relevant information up front, journalists work almost exclusively with open questions when on the job.

Therefore, in the business environment, if you are looking for information, think like a journalist and use exclusively open questions. Encourage the other person to talk so you can create your own lead for the situation at hand.

Physicians: Moving from Open to Closed

Now think about what happens when you are shown into a capable doctor's examining room. The doctor walks in, looks you right in the eye, approaches you directly, and shakes your hand.

The doctor is already beginning to collect information. By looking in your eyes, he or she can glean information about your health. The reason for the handshake is not so much that the doctor is being friendly, but is actually a test to see how firm your grip is and how moist the palm of the hand is.

Then the doctor asks a series of open questions: "How are you feeling?" "Why are you here today?" "What seems to be the problem?" These open questions are designed to draw out general information about your symptoms.

Once the doctor has asked enough open questions to come up with a few possible diagnoses, he or she will start using closed questions to eliminate possibilities and treat you accordingly.

Therefore, when you need to diagnose a problem with an employee, start with open questions, then progress to closed questions to narrow it down.

———

In summary, closed questions tend to generate short answers with little additional information, while open questions tend to provide more information, making it easier to diagnose a problem and identify an effective solution. Both closed and open questions have important places in business; leaders need to know when to use each type to promote effective communication.

"I suppose I was in too much of a hurry at the end of the meeting," said Frank thoughtfully.

"Just at the end of the meeting?" asked his grandmother with a raised eyebrow.

Frank looked at her blankly. "What?"

His grandmother sighed. "Frankie, communication is about giving and receiving information. You're always in too much of a rush to do either well. You've got to slow down and put more thought into it."

"I don't have time! You have no idea how fast business moves today!"

"Trust me on this, Frankie. If you slow down, your progress will speed up."

The Johari Window

Let's break communication into its component parts. For that, we turn to a model known as the Johari Window.

The Johari Window was developed by Joseph Luft and Harrington Ingham (Joe and Harry, hence, "Johari"). Their research showed that the "window" of communication has two axes, or two "directions":

1. The vertical axis is called *exposure*. This is when we make a deliberate and conscious attempt to let another person know what is going on inside our heads by conveying both facts and feelings.

2. The horizontal axis is called *feedback*. This is when we make a deliberate and conscious attempt to find out what is in someone else's head and elicit feedback *from* them. And again, this is on both the factual level and the feeling level.

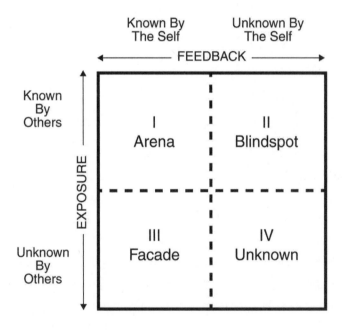

By changing your level of exposure and feedback, you increase or decrease the amount of information that you have and others have, thereby affecting the relative size of the four quadrants of the window. Luft and Ingham posited that the most effective communication takes place when there is a large amount of both exposure and feedback. An ideal amount is about 80 percent of the maximum for each. Here is what this looks like:

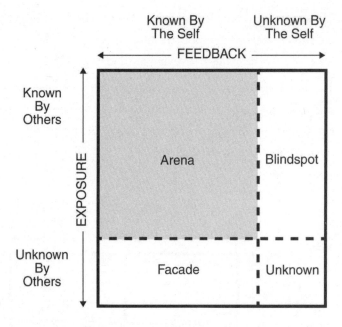

In this window, exposure and feedback have optimized the amount of information that is known to self and others. In other words, everyone has the important facts, everyone knows where each party is coming from emotionally, everyone understands the data, and everyone is clear on the direction.

In using the Johari Window, it's vital to remember that communication always takes place on those two levels: facts and feelings. To focus exclusively on one or the other is to inhibit full communication.

The Johari Window is particularly helpful in achieving effective communication because it reminds us graphically that, in any situation, we start with a lot of unknowns. We may have facts that the others don't have. They may be thinking or feeling things that we have no awareness of. We may not even know what we don't know about a situation. It is by deliberately and consciously increasing exposure and feedback that we lessen those unknowns.

The other point that the Johari Window makes is that full responsibility for the success of communication lies with you. You are responsible for 100 percent of the information you share and for 100 percent of the information you receive. Excuses such as "They didn't tell me," "I didn't know," or "She should have asked" don't fly here. It is entirely your responsibility to provide data, elicit information, and check for understanding.

Frank got up and began to pace by the fireplace. He ran a hand along the mantel. "It's frustrating, you know. In other aspects of business, you have clear deliverables. Make this. Do that. Process these numbers. Call those people. But when you talk to people, how do you know if you're going about it right? It's all so nebulous."

"Stuff and nonsense!" scoffed his grandmother. "You look at words as intangible, therefore ungovernable. But that's ridiculous. Numbers are intangible, but you have accountants on staff. Satisfaction is intangible, but you hire customer service representatives. The point is, you have determined the rules and elements that lead to successful accounting and to successful service. Do the same here—the only difference is, you are the communicator. You can't pass this responsibility off to someone else."

Opening the Communication Window

There are ten key ways to increase the amount and effectiveness of your exposure—that is, what you share with others—as you open a Johari Window of communication:

1. **Describe the situation and your reactions.** As we said earlier, avoid making assumptions about what the other person knows. Take the time to make sure the person you are speaking with knows what is going on and understands your perspective on the situation.

2. **Don't assume you know what the other person is thinking or feeling.** If you assume you know what is going on inside another person's head or heart, that may affect what information you share with them. You're not a mind reader; don't make assumptions.

3. **Don't judge a person's character.** If you consider a person to be worthless or lazy or stupid, you will limit your exposure to that person, potentially limiting their effectiveness on the job. If you consider a person to be a saint or capable of walking on water (what we call the "halo effect"), you may give them more information than they need to be successful.

4. **Be specific in what you say.** As you share information with others, avoid generalities. Don't assume the other person knows or understands what you are talking about. Give concrete examples to demonstrate your points.

5. **Give information rather than advice.** People feel patronized if you preach at them. They tend to stop listening and will refuse to give you feedback about themselves. Instead, focus on factual information they can use.

6. **Keep in mind the receiver's needs, not your own.** When we communicate, we can become fond of the sound of our own voices. But much of communication is really about the other person. Keep your focus on the other person: their reactions, their feedback, and their comprehension.

7. **Check for understanding.** Don't simply ask, "Do you understand?" (a closed question that will almost always result in a yes, regardless of actual understanding). Instead, ask open questions such as "What is your understanding of what we have agreed to?" "How would that translate into your job?" or "How would that work for you?"

8. **Keep in mind how much the receiver can handle and use.** Engaging in an information dump is not necessarily a good communication technique. You may think you are increasing exposure by

pouring out the facts, but if the receiver can't assimilate the material, you are actually lowering the amount of exposure through information overload.

9.   **Level with the receiver; don't level the receiver.** If you have to deliver unpleasant news, be factual and unemotional. For instance, state calmly, "Due to the rising cost of doing business, we will have to raise member dues," rather than snapping, "Can't you understand that we can't run this operation on a shoestring!"

10.   **Maintain your sense of humor.** Be willing to laugh—especially at yourself! You can lighten a tense moment by interjecting a little humor and can strengthen personal connections by demonstrating the humility necessary to poke a little fun at yourself.

What do these rules look like in action? Consider the manufacturing supervisor who needs to approach one of his employees—we'll call him Joe—for being verbally abusive to coworkers. The manager catches Joe one morning by the water cooler and says, "You know, Joe, I think mutual respect is important for the team's well-being, don't you?"

Joe agrees wholeheartedly. Heartened, the manager continues, "How we say things really contributes to feelings of respect, don't you think?" Again, Joe concurs. The manager returns to his office, satisfied that he has addressed the issue. Joe returns to the line and promptly berates one of his coworkers.

What happened? The manager broke several of the above rules of exposure. First, he didn't describe the situation and his reactions. He didn't say, for example, "Joe, several of your coworkers have reported that you raise your voice and use inappropriate and abusive language toward them on a regular basis. I am very concerned about this, because verbal abuse will not be tolerated in this organization."

Second, the manager wasn't specific. He didn't say, "I want you to be respectful in your language at all times. This means you don't raise your voice, you don't use expletives, and you don't attack your coworkers, regardless of what you may perceive as provocation."

Finally, the manager assumed he knew what Joe was thinking and feeling, so he didn't check for understanding. He didn't ask, "How do you intend to change your behavior toward your coworkers?" He assumed that Joe knew what he was referring to by his detached, third-person speech about mutual respect, so he never asked Joe to paraphrase back to him what had been said. If he had, the manager might have caught on to the fact that his generalities had flown completely past Joe.

Frank sat down suddenly and leaned forward, elbows on his knees. "Grandma, tell me. How do you always know what to say and how to say it?"

She looked at him thoughtfully. "I just listen, Frankie."

"I listen to people all the time, but I don't have the insights you do. I don't seem to make the connection. To be candid, I stick my foot in my mouth on a regular basis—but I never realize it until I've got the taste of shoe leather on my tongue."

"You say you listen, but you really don't, Frankie." Her tone was gentle. "What you call 'listening' is really 'waiting for an opportunity to speak.' Until you get past yourself, you'll never be able to listen well."

Listening Well

The single greatest key to increasing the amount and effectiveness of the feedback you receive—and to improving your communication on the whole—is to listen. Pure and simple.

Unfortunately, most listening is not pure, and effective listening is not simple. There are four types of listening that we can engage in:

1. Physical Listening

With this type of listening, we are bodily present but not really paying much attention to what is going on. We often use this style when we are speaking with someone who is nonthreatening or with someone we don't take seriously, and/or when we are absolutely overwhelmed and distracted.

An excellent example of physical listening comes from the 1964 movie *Mary Poppins*, when George Banks's wife tells him that their children are missing. He is so consumed with his own needs that he simply is not listening. As he walks about the house, singing about the consistency and reliability of his home life, the pleasures of punctuality and his "slippers, sherry, and pipe," his wife trails him, desperately trying to break through and explain that the children are gone. Yet Mr. Banks remains oblivious, offering rote affirmations—"Splendid, splendid"—to his wife before continuing his self-focused song.

2. Tape Listening

This is a little bit better than physical listening. We're not really interested in what the other person is saying, but we feel we need to attend on some level. If asked for our understanding of what was said, we'll repeat it back word for word as if we're playing back a tape of the conversation.

We all do this from time to time. How many times have you repeated exactly what your spouse said to you but had no idea what he or she meant? This is tape listening at its worst.

3. Judgmental Listening

We slip into this type of listening when emotions are running high. The conversation becomes a win/lose scenario. We are not listening to comprehend; we're listening to hone our rebuttal, often formulating a response in our heads while the other person is talking. Judgmental listening can look like dueling monologues.

Tuning into any political talk show on cable television will give you a great example of judgmental listening.

4. Active Listening

Our objective in active (or empathic) listening is to understand what the other person is saying. Note: the goal is understanding, not necessarily *agreement*. If we're practicing active listening, there is usually an open, two-way dialogue in progress.

Active listening is vital to establishing healthy relationships. In active listening, you are 100 percent present with the other person, demonstrating your respect for them, for their views, and for their feelings. As a result, though you may not agree at the end, you can still move forward. For example, suppose your business is in crunch mode, and long overtime hours will be necessary to keep production up to speed. Your employees are unhappy about this. If you actively listen to their concerns and feelings, they're still not going to be happy about doing the overtime, but they will be *willing* to do it because they know that you respect them and share their concerns. You have strengthened your relationship and therefore strengthened your business.

There are two particularly useful tools when it comes to active listening: paraphrasing and reflection.

Paraphrasing deals with the content of a conversation: the facts, figures, events, and issues at hand. When you paraphrase, you deliver an accurate, neutral summary of the key data in the conversation. You want to demonstrate understanding, not necessarily agreement or disagreement. Be brief: you are recapping the conversation, not playing it back verbatim.

Reflection deals with the emotions involved in a conversation. Here, you reflect back to the receiver what you are hearing about their feelings, e.g., "That must make you frustrated" or "It sounds like you're at the end of your rope." Through reflection, you show that you understand and respect a person's emotions. In tense situations, reflection can take you from being the person's adversary to becoming the person's advocate. It often helps both parties move past the emotion to a calmer discussion of the issue at hand.

The key to the success of both paraphrasing and reflection statements is not to sound "technique-y" or condescending. If you sound like you are talking to a two-year-old, your business associates or employ-ees will feel deeply offended and patronized. Let your honest desire for true understanding and connection come through your voice and your body language.

As a final note, active listening, paraphrasing, and reflection are more than communication tools for leaders: they are also problem solvers. For example, one manager we worked with had a team member who con-stantly complained about the work habits of the people who sat near her. The manager had tried moving her desk to different locations, putting up partitions, and other methods of solving the problem, but nothing worked: the complaints continued.

We suggested that he use a reflection statement with her, so the next time she was ranting in his office, he said, "It must be incredibly frustrat-ing for you. I know how dedicated you are to doing the job right." She immediately calmed down and agreed. From that point on, she was a much less frequent visitor to the manager's office.

Had anything changed in the office? No. But reflection had caused something to change inside *her*. She felt heard, and because she felt heard, she was more willing to deal well with her coworkers. Using a reflection statement contributed to the solution.

Frank looked at his watch and started. "Grandma, I'm sorry!" he apolo-gized. "I've got to head for home. I've got an all-staff meeting tomorrow, and I still have to get a PowerPoint presentation together."

"No, Frankie."

Frank paused in the act of standing up. He sank back into the chair. "What?"

"You don't have to get a PowerPoint presentation together. You hide behind those slides or whatever you call them, and you just end up talk-ing. You need to communicate with your team. That means you can't just tell them what you have to say. You have to listen for their input as well. And don't you forget it!"

Communicating to Groups

As a business leader, you must remember that communication to groups follows the same principles as those we've discussed for one-on-one communication. It doesn't matter whether the group is composed of ten VPs or a thousand shareholders. Your goals remain the same: to communicate information, promote understanding, and establish connections.

When communicating to groups, it is wise to keep several points in mind:

Charisma can never replace preparation. A lot of leaders rely on their personal charisma when it comes to speaking to a group. They trust that they will know what to say in the moment and that their personality will carry them through. However, no matter how dynamic your personality is, you will always be more effective with solid preparation. Identify the goals of your communication, organize your main points to support those goals, sketch out your supporting information, and determine the plan of action you want people to take. Until you can talk fluently from a set of bullet points, take the time to write out your entire speech or presentation. If you practice it several times, you will not need to refer to your notes extensively in the actual event, but you will have your script in front of you should you need it.

Stories are powerful. You may have a very limited number of opportunities to speak to a large group, such as a shareholder meeting or an all-staff meeting. You want to be as effective as possible. If you speak in generalities or fall back on quoting financials or other statistics, your audience's eyes will glaze over. To effectively communicate your vision or objective, make it real with a story or two. People love stories (even in the business setting!), and great storytelling goes hand in hand with great leadership.

Anticipate feedback. If the group setting prevents asking for on-the-spot feedback, you have to anticipate that feedback and incorporate it proactively into your content. Go over your presentation with several people before you deliver it, and have them ask you the toughest questions possible. Then, go back and work the answers to those questions into your presentation.

Whether you are speaking to an individual or to a group, be sure to treat people as *people*. They are not tools, resources, or a headcount. They will always bring to the table their opinions, emotions, perspectives, and life experiences. If you want to communicate effectively with others, you need to respect them as human beings.

"I won't forget, Grandma," said Frank, rising to his feet. "I've been listening."

"Now that would be a change," replied his grandmother tartly. But she smiled.

INSPIRING ENGAGEMENT: *MOTIVATION*

Frank opened the door to his grandmother's house with a sigh of frustration. His grandmother looked up from her seat at the dining room table where she was polishing the silver and raised an eyebrow. "Bad day?" she asked in a neutral tone.

"The worst."

"Take off your coat and come sit down."

Frank did so, stopping briefly in the kitchen to pour himself a glass of iced tea.

She gestured to the table. "Make yourself useful."

Frank picked up one of the silver-polishing cloths. For a few minutes, he burnished a silver creamer in silence. "These new dry wipes are certainly easier than the old blue goop you used to use."

His grandmother wasn't fooled. "Tell me what happened."

"Jarrod resigned."

The announcement made both of his grandmother's eyebrows go up. "Your VP of finance?"

"Yep."

"You were friends!"

"I thought we were."

"Well, what did he say?"

"That he was bored. He was fed up with shuffling papers and putting out fires. He said he just felt sick and tired inside." Frank's voice was sad. "I didn't see it. I never knew."

"I understand, Frankie," said his grandmother gently. "It's a real worry when even your best people are just going through the motions."

Engagement on the Decline

There is a crisis of engagement and motivation today in the American workforce. This isn't a feeling or a suspicion or an unfounded fear. It is a fact. Gallup routinely measures employee engagement across the nation, and their findings are sobering:

- **Only 28 percent of American employees are engaged on the job.** Engaged workers exhibit a strong emotional and rational commitment to their day-to-day work, the manager, the team, and the organization. They display a willingness to help others with heavy workloads, volunteer for extra responsibilities, and constantly look for ways to improve their performance.

- **54 percent of the workforce is disengaged.** Disengaged employees show up to work each day and do the minimum to get by. They collect a paycheck and go home. They lack emotional commitment and passion for their work.

- **18 percent, or nearly 1 in 5 American employees, are *actively* disengaged in their jobs.** Actively disengaged individuals display lack of commitment to the company's future and are opposed to just about everything. They are often miserable, and they share their complaints and bitterness with anyone who will listen. In fact, they recruit new people to "their side" every day.

Put this information together, and it means that 74 percent of American workers are either disengaged or actively disengaged in their jobs. The result? "The lower productivity of actively disengaged workers costs the

US economy about $382 billion annually."[7] That's a pretty dire situation that the complete leader must handle effectively.

There was silence for a few minutes as the two sat quietly polishing the silver. "I notice that you're not angry, Frankie," said his grandmother tentatively.

Frank shrugged. "I was. Briefly. When he walked out of my office after handing me his letter of resignation, I wanted to blame him and tell him 'good riddance.' But it's not good riddance. He's a great man and he's going to leave a big hole." He paused. "I feel like I failed him somehow."

"Perhaps you did."

Frank turned tormented eyes toward her. "But what could I have done? I can't reach inside him to make him feel better, can I? I can't give him back the enthusiasm he once had. The joy. The fire. That's got to come from within."

"Yes, it does, Frankie. But you can fan the flames."

Inspiring Motivation and Engagement from the Outside

Referring to Gallup's employee engagement data, Clint Swindall observes, "Most leaders find a way to blame this crisis of disengagement on the employee, but the responsibility for productivity and profitability rests entirely on the shoulders of leadership, and so does the responsibility for the overcoming of employee disengagement."[8]

Put simply, employee engagement and motivation come from within, but they must be consistently encouraged from without.

How can leaders fan the flames of motivation and engagement? It begins with an understanding of why people act the way they do. In a nutshell, here is the ultimate explanation for all human behavior (well, maybe not quite that all-encompassing, but close to it!):

1. As long as we are breathing, we all have *needs*.

2. Our *goal* is to get those needs met. This is our motivating force in life.

3. Our *behavior* is guided by our efforts to get our needs met and thereby reach our goal.

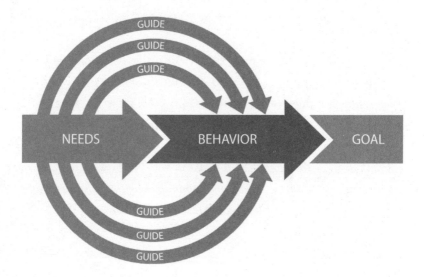

The strangest behaviors usually become completely understandable once we recognize the need that is driving a person and the goal they are trying to reach. Everyone behaves in ways that make sense to them.

Take the director who calls her direct reports at home at midnight to have them make changes to a slide deck. Why? The changes are minor. In fact, they are mostly stylistic—made to incorporate her style. The reason? The director has two key needs: a fanatical desire to look good in front of the CEO, who would be seeing the slide deck the following day, and a tremendous sense of perfectionism that demanded she put her own stamp on anything coming from her office. Given those needs, her behavior is completely understandable, even if it could be considered unacceptable by others.

To create a culture of motivation and engagement, you as a leader need to understand what people's needs are in the workplace so that you can help them achieve their goals. Certainly, people will have needs that cannot be met in the workplace (e.g., the desire for marriage or to have a child), but a huge number of people's needs can be addressed from nine to five, Monday through Friday.

However, an immediate problem surfaces: people don't walk around with their needs written on their foreheads or emblazoned across their clothes. Where do you begin to identify and address those needs?

"I try to create the right corporate culture, Grandma, I really do. I give my people great salaries and an unbeatable benefit package. If they do their job well, they've got job security. What more can people want?"

His grandmother polished a fork, inspected its tines carefully, and laid it in the velvet-lined case. Without looking up she said, "Frankie, what if I got you a job tomorrow at a fish cannery?"

"What!" Frank stared at her in disbelief.

"Yes, I know you hate even the smell of fish. But wouldn't packing the slimy, stinking, slippery fish for eight hours a day be worth it if I promised you double your current salary, a substantial 401(k) contribution, and no chance of a layoff—even in the event of a recession?"

"Grandma, nothing could make me work in a fish cannery. Period."

"Why not? How about packing chocolates at our local plant instead? You like chocolate well enough," she said wickedly.

He glared at her good-naturedly. "No."

"Again, why not?"

"You're serious, aren't you?"

"For the sake of argument, yes."

Frank set down the silver cloth. "Because working in a factory would bore me to tears."

"You worked in a factory after college and were glad for the job."

"It was different back then."

"Ah," said his grandmother, a twinkle in her eye. "So money and

benefits and security aren't enough for you now. You want something more. You know, I don't think you're alone in that, Frankie."

The Hierarchy of Needs

In the 1940s, a psychologist named Abraham Maslow did pioneering work that helped us understand the developmental nature of human needs. He proposed a model—the hierarchy of needs—that would revolutionize our understanding of human motivation.

Though trained as a psychologist, Maslow came to be regarded as a management theorist as well. His hierarchy-of-needs model remains a fundamental component of many psychology courses. Here, however, we will look at its specific, practical, and results-oriented application to organizations.

Maslow's model is typically represented as a pyramid:

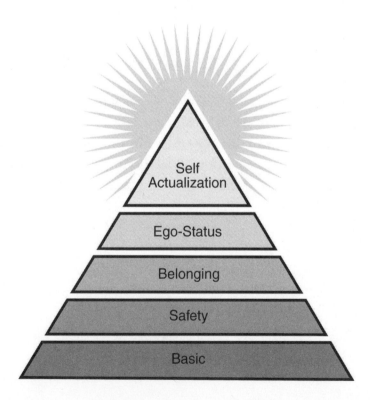

At the bottom of the pyramid are our *basic needs*: food, shelter, clothing—everything you need to survive. In business, employers provide for basic needs by issuing a paycheck.

The next level represents our *security needs*: orderliness and safety. We want to make sure our home, health, family, and job are secure. Companies meet their employees' security needs through such things as health insurance, benefits, human resource policies, safety regulations, and retirement programs.

In the middle of the pyramid stand our *belonging needs*. With the basics for survival met and made secure, we begin to look outside ourselves and find a new set of needs. These needs can be characterized by a set of questions, including these:

1.   Do I like the people I work with?

2.   Do I feel like I am part of a team here?

3.   Am I accepted and respected in this group?

4.   Do I sense camaraderie on the job?

Belonging needs are often overlooked in companies because the focus is on getting the job done. But the fact is, you can get the job done, get paid well for your work, be secure in your position, and still be very unmotivated because you are lacking relationships and connectedness within the organization.

So how can organizations meet people's belonging needs? These needs can be met directly *within* the corporate environment, and through extracurricular activities sponsored by the corporate leadership. You could, for instance,

- **Increase internal communications** to let employees know they are a part of a larger whole. For example, a company can let people know true-life stories of the positive changes their products are producing in people's lives.

- **Celebrate events within departments,** such as having a monthly birthday party or recognition for various career milestones.

- **Create cross-functional teams** to oversee specific work initiatives. Empower these teams with resources, decision-making power, and the ability to implement their strategies.

- **Encourage activities outside the office,** such as social events, holiday parties, or athletic teams.

- **Engage in team-building exercises** within your leadership. This does not mean sitting around a campfire singing "Kumbaya," nor does it mean doing the old trust fall! Real team-building events are strategic in nature and business focused, and they reap practical rewards when leaders are back in the office. For example, hold a training session based on leadership behavioral profiles of team members, such as DiSC® or Myers-Briggs Type Indicator®.

- **Sponsor community outreach projects** and give people time off from work to participate personally. Such projects could vary from participating in a fund-raising walk or race to repainting a local homeless shelter. Track the number of people who get involved and how much time they commit to the project. And then celebrate that volunteerism internally. You may even want to issue a press release to applaud employee efforts.

- **Support spontaneous team development.** Teams will sometimes arise spontaneously within the business as like-minded people bond together to work on a mutual concern. Some leaders feel threatened when this happens. Don't be! Embrace these teams, because they usually have an energy and innovation level that is second to none. Take full advantage of this internal momentum by backing the team with resources and strategic assistance. Then stand back and watch them deliver!

Interestingly, once people have their belonging needs met by feeling part of a team, group, or community, the next level of need is the need to stand out. People want to know that they are special: that they have skills, talents, insights, and expertise that enable them to make their own unique contribution to the organization. This is called an *ego need*.

The word *ego* has developed a bad rap over the years, so it needs to be understood in context. When Maslow first used the term, it simply meant the need to stand out and be recognized. It had nothing to do with arrogance, inappropriate pride, or self-centeredness.

Businesses meet employee's ego needs through advancement, appreciation, rewards, and acknowledgement. This doesn't sound so hard, and it isn't, in theory. In practice, it is another matter. In a 2003 study, five thousand employees were asked, "What is the first thing your immediate supervisor said to you when you completed your last major project?" A full 94 percent said that the supervisor said nothing.[9] *Nothing!*

Ouch! So much for appreciation, reward, and acknowledgement. It's little wonder that many employees feel that their ego needs are being swept into the dustbin.

When team members perform well, you as a leader might think, "But that's their job! Why should I reward them just for doing their job?" The answer to that question depends on whether you want engaged employees or dissatisfied drones. If you want engagement, learn to thank, praise, celebrate, and reward your employees.

And bear in mind, meeting people's ego needs can have a very long-lasting effect. We once worked with a senior corporate officer who told a great story about the lasting effect of meeting ego level needs. Here's what Joe has to say:

"I was attending the company holiday party. Having been in the organization only four months, I was still feeling my way carefully through the projects, the politics, and the people. At the party, one of the division heads buttonholed me, pulled me over to the CEO, and said, 'Boss, I have to tell you, in four months, Joe has us thinking about things we never thought of before. I can't tell you how much of a difference he has made to our business!' That was 1995, and I am still telling this story and feeling that rush of pride."

This coworker met Joe's ego needs tenfold, and it didn't take him long to do it—probably less than two minutes total. You can bet that Joe gave his colleague 100 percent effort every time he worked with him from that point forward.

When ego needs have been met, energy is freed up and people begin to move to the highest level of need attainment: *self-actualization needs.*

When we self-actualize, we tap into our deepest skills and highest abilities. It is at this point that our potential becomes reality. We prove ourselves to ourselves by testing our capabilities and pushing ourselves to perform at the highest possible level. It is here, at the pinnacle of Maslow's hierarchy of needs, that motivation is at its peak, satisfaction is at its highest, and performance is at its best.

To satisfy ego needs, we often need extrinsic motivators like promotion, recognition, and reward, but at the self-actualization level, motivation becomes entirely intrinsic. We do what we do because we are passionate about it. Self-actualization is living out our "actual self." Once we reach that place, there is no turning back.

In the business world, a leader cannot simply flip a switch and cause his or her people to be self-actualized, but he or she can pay very close attention to people in order to discover what makes them tick. If self-actualization occurs within the job, there's no limit to what the person can accomplish for the company. Listen closely to what people are passionate about. Pay attention to the things they talk about. Ask them what they are most interested in and what they want to accomplish in their work. Once you become fully aware of your people's hopes, dreams, and passions, concentrate on helping them reach those goals. Your people and your business will prosper.

For example, a bank's lending division hired a young man who had a passion for the written word. But he was hired to make cold sales calls. The VP two levels up from the young man, however, knew of his strong internal drive to write. Therefore, when the VP saw an ad for a national financial conference's essay contest, he called the young man into his office. He explained that the winner of the essay contest would have an all-expenses-paid trip to the conference, a cash award, public recognition at the conference, and publication in a major trade journal.

The young man spent the next month interviewing bankers, attorneys, and accountants on retail bankruptcy—and wrote the winning essay. His award gave him exposure to the chairman and CEO of one of the nation's largest banks, and the magazine cover showing his name hung in his office during his entire long, successful, and satisfying career as an executive VP in banking.

The Dynamics of Need

The complete leader must understand three dynamics that are at play when considering people's needs:

- *Dynamic #1:* **Progression.** People do not move haphazardly from level to level. They don't skip down from belonging to basic and then shoot up to ego needs. Instead, people move from the bottom up in an orderly, step-by-step progression. Basic survival needs must be met first. If you don't have these basic needs met, you can't focus on any of the other, higher-level needs in the pyramid. When our basic needs are met, energy is freed up to pursue security needs. From there, people move on to their belonging needs. And so on.

- *Dynamic #2:* **Fulfillment.** Once a need has been fulfilled, what happens? We are satisfied, but only temporarily. We quickly turn our attention to other needs. And here is the key that Maslow realized: *once a given need is fulfilled, it no longer motivates.* This is the reason that throwing more money at someone will not make them more motivated. If their basic and security needs have already been met, money simply isn't the need that is driving them. To motivate them, you have to speak to their new level of need.

- *Dynamic #3:* **Frustration.** Frustration causes more problems for more leaders than any other dynamic. If people have particular needs on the job and nothing on the job is helping to address those needs, what effect does that have on behavior? The answer: they complain. But what do they complain about? *They complain about a lower level of need.* People don't complain about what's really bothering them—perhaps because they feel too vulnerable in that area. So they complain about something else—some need that has already been met.

"You're right," said Frank thoughtfully. "In fact, my needs have changed several times. Just out of college, a paycheck was enough. Then I got the job at the electronics firm. That let me collaborate with others and bring a new product to market. That made me positively heady—I loved it! I wanted to do it all the time."

"So you opened your own business to let you do what you loved."

"Yes. That was the primary reason. Odd, I'd almost forgotten."

"Don't forget it," his grandmother warned gently. "You have something most people only dream about."

6 Motivation Mistakes

Now that we've looked at each level of Maslow's hierarchy of needs and how businesses can meet them, it is time to make some very practical observations about where motivation most commonly goes wrong. Here are the top six motivation mistakes we see in our work with leaders:

Mistake #1: Believing that motivation comes exclusively from within

Well, yes and no. Motivation ultimately does come from within. But as a leader, you can create an atmosphere in which motivation flourishes. You can do so by

- making sure people's basic survival needs are met;
- providing a secure working environment;
- fostering a team-oriented attitude;

- taking the time to appreciate what people do; and

- enabling people where possible to reach their highest self-actualizing goals.

So yes, motivation does come from within. But no, that doesn't let you off the hook as a leader.

Mistake #2: Believing that your motivational efforts by themselves will transform people

This is the flip side of the first mistake. Yes, you can do many things that will foster a culture of motivation. However, you can do all the right things and people can remain cynical, skeptical, bitter, and disengaged. That is a hard reality, but it is reality nonetheless.

Additionally, you can't motivate solely by the force of your personality, or by inspirational speeches, or by demanding that people become engaged. The sooner you accept this fact, the faster you can move on to focusing your energy where it will give you the greatest return.

Mistake #3: Believing that money equals motivation

We've said it already, but it is worth repeating: money only motivates at the level of basic needs. Once basic needs have been met, money is far, far less of a motivator. Does that mean you never have to give people raises after their basic needs have been met? No, it does not. While money may cease to motivate people after a certain point, if you don't compensate people appropriately, you will quickly *de-motivate* them.

You may be thinking, "Surely if the dollar amount is big enough, anybody would be motivated!" Not true. We were once hired by a successful entrepreneur who asked us to help him grow his business to the next level. In discussions with him, we learned that he began his career in commercial banking. Here's what he told us: "Each year, I would receive a substantial year-end bonus. I discovered that a nice amount of money did not make me feel fulfilled in my work. In truth, I was miserable in my job. One year, on February 28, the bonus showed up via direct deposit in my bank account, over $20,000. I looked at the number, smiled briefly, and went back to being miserable. When I left the bank to start my own company, I obviously took a tremendous cut in income. But my motivation soared. The money didn't matter nearly as much as the fun I was having in my work. Why? Because I found building a business to be fulfilling, enjoyable, and energizing." Our friend was desperate to have his self-actualization needs met. When they were, he prospered. We have seen this happen with many clients, who have found ways to challenge team members with new assignments that stretch their abilities. Those team members have stayed with their companies and prospered as well.

Mistake #4: Believing what people tell you

We are not saying that people regularly lie about what does and doesn't make them feel engaged and motivated at work—far from it. But sometimes they may not know themselves what's really bothering them, or they may be unwilling to admit it. This ties into the dynamic of frustration we spoke of earlier: when a person has a particular need, he or she complains instead about a need from one of the lower levels of the pyramid.

Therefore, when people complain to you, take some time to ask a few questions and find out what is really bothering them. Are they truly upset about the issue at hand, or is something more going on? Consider the following examples:

- You hear that your line supervisor is griping about his salary. Considering that he was recently promoted, you think this is a bit strange. You then realize that in the course of his promotion, he was transferred to a new facility. He may actually be suffering from not having his *belonging needs* met because he has not yet become integrated into his new group.

- Your marketing director resigns. In her exit interview, she tells HR that she "didn't fit into the corporate culture." What she was really saying was that she had received no recognition for her hard work and top performance on recent projects. She decided to take her talents where they would be appreciated. So while she pointed to belonging needs, it was unfulfilled ego needs that caused her to leave.

- Your vice president has become disengaged in his work. When pressed about his change of behavior, he says he feels bored and asks, "Is this all there is?" Yet you always make it a point to let your senior staff know how much you value them. Your vice president is likely being stymied by unmet self-actualization needs. His work is no longer challenging or fulfilling and he feels like he is not making a difference in the company.

How will you know where the truth is? The better you know your people and the safer they feel with you, the more likely they are to tell you the truth. But if you aren't sure—or if they aren't sure—ask some open questions (ones that require more than a yes or no in response) relating to the various levels of need. For example you might ask, "In the past year, where do you feel you made the greatest contribution?" and "What was most fulfilling about your work?" and "As you think about our company's goals in the next year, what would you most like to focus on?"

Mistake #5: Assuming that you already know what motivates people

We have seen a number of surveys that draw a fascinating distinction between what managers think their employees want at work and what employees actually do want. These surveys often generate similar answers. When managers are asked, "What is most important to your employees?" the top answers are often:

1. Salary

2. Benefits

3. Job security

On the other hand, when employees are asked, "What is important to you?" their answers differ significantly:

1. Challenging work

2. Recognition for a job well done

3. A sense of being "in the know"

This shows how easy it is to misunderstand what motivates your people. Be careful with your assumptions.

Mistake #6: Underestimating the profound impact motivation has on your business

What does employee motivation really accomplish for your business? Leaders who actively engage in creating an environment where motivation can flourish see the following effects:

- they are two times more likely to complete projects on time, on budget, and with the highest-quality standards;

- they enjoy an employee engagement rate of 83 percent;

- they show a 12.5 percent increase in productivity; and

- they experience a 9.8 percent increase in profitability.[10]

The moral of the story? Motivation matters.

Frank put the last of the cutlery in the polished wooden box and closed the lid with a click. "I'm worried, Grandma."

"About . . . ?"

"I'm wondering if anyone else is feeling the way Jarrod felt. I'm wondering if I'm going to lose more people because of mistakes I've made without even knowing it."

His grandmother's voice was gentle. "Don't worry about making mistakes, Frankie. Worrying is a waste of energy. Pour all that effort into correcting them, and you'll be just fine."

GUIDING BEHAVIOR: *FEEDBACK*

"*What are you working on so diligently, Frankie?*" *inquired his grand-mother. She had come in for a fresh cup of tea, and poured the steaming brew carefully into a delicate china cup etched with rosebuds.*

Frank looked up from his laptop on the kitchen table. "*It's annual review time.*" *He grimaced.* "*Everybody's least favorite time of year.*"

"*Why is that?*"

"*Well, if you have direct reports, you either have the pleasant task of giving them a handshake and a bonus check, or the unpleasant task of tell-ing them their work isn't up to par. And if you're on the other side of the desk, you are on tenterhooks until you know which the outcome is going to be. Everybody's tense as all get-out.*"

"*But, Frankie,*" *said his grandmother, slightly puzzled,* "*doesn't every-body know how they're doing already?*"

The Power of Feedback

Feedback is perhaps the single most powerful tool the complete leader has at his or her disposal to bring about significant improvement in employee engagement and performance. In the last chapter we described Maslow's hierarchy of needs, and feedback supports all the hierarchy's upper levels—it can increase feelings of belonging, satisfy ego needs, and reinforce the drive for self-actualization. Leadership expert Rick Tate wisely noted that "feedback is the breakfast of champions."[11]

That being said, what exactly is feedback? Unfortunately, people often have very few positive examples on which to draw. Many of us have even been "abused" by poorly given feedback and still sting from the experience. Here's our definition of good feedback—the kind that helps rather than hurts:

> **Feedback is having an open and honest two-way conversation about performance that is specific in its nature and clearly defines future desired behaviors.**

Consider each part of that definition carefully:

- When it is *open and honest*, feedback improves communication between the two parties and validates the employee.

- If it is truly a *two-way conversation*, feedback increases mutual respect between the two parties, improves understanding of how each person thinks and approaches situations, and fosters productive collaboration.

- When it is *directed at performance issues*, feedback clarifies exactly what the employee is doing incorrectly or ineffectively and increases the employee's sense of ownership of the situation.

- By being *specific in its nature*, feedback increases the employee's understanding of the ramifications of his or her behavior.

- By being *clear about future desired behaviors*, feedback makes it far more likely that the employee can be effective in his or her role.

The positive outcomes of giving effective feedback are astonishing and oftentimes bring about company-wide improvements. Effective feedback can

- increase productivity,

- increase sales and improve the bottom line,

- decrease conflict,

- streamline processes,

- increase creativity,

- improve delegation,

- improve efficiency,

- uncover training needs,

- improve customer service,

- help people develop new skills, and

- improve problem-solving abilities.

We consider feedback to be one of the most important and powerful leadership tools you can develop. In fact, when we are asked to list the most important leadership skills, effectively giving feedback is always near the top of the list.

"I suppose in general terms people know how they're doing," said Frank with a shrug.

His grandmother sat down deliberately at the table, and something in her attitude told Frank that he was in trouble. "Let me get this straight, Frankie. Your people—up and down the line—go all year without a clue as to what they're doing right and what they're doing wrong, and then you either crown them with laurels or cut off their heads in their annual review?"

"It's not that bad," Frank said lamely.

"Knowing your gift for understatement, it's probably worse," replied his grandmother in an acid tone. "So answer me this. Do you—and all your cronies, because I'm not letting any of you off the hook here—act in this irresponsible fashion because you don't know any better, or because you don't know how to do better? And before you answer, let me tell you that ignorance is no excuse, either way!"

Why Leaders Don't Give Feedback

If feedback has so many benefits, why don't leaders give it more often? Most of the time, the excuses (notice that they are not reasons—they are excuses) fall into six general categories:

Excuse #1: "Why should I?"

This first excuse is most often given when talking about *reinforcing feedback*: that is, feedback that recognizes a job well done and seeks to encourage repeat behavior.

We have heard leaders say, "I'm paying these people to work! Why should I have to tell them they're doing a good job all the time?"

Our response to this old-school philosophy is this: Imagine you're in the stadium watching your favorite team and they score. What do you do? You yell and cheer and wave your arms, along with thousands of other people! Why are you doing that? The members of that team are being paid (often outrageous sums of money). They're just doing their job! Do they need you to cheer?

But you do cheer them—time and again. Why? Because you are giving them positive, reinforcing feedback. You want them to know that you're behind them, supporting them, rooting for them. Employees have the same needs!

Excuse #2: "No news is good news."

The second excuse is closely allied with the first but deserves to be addressed directly. It is the idea that "Well, I may not be saying anything positive, but I'm not saying anything negative, so people should know they're okay." In this case, the leader believes that the only feedback that needs to be stated directly is negative feedback. This is the corporate spin on the old joke: a wife is tearfully asking her husband if he loves her and he replies irritably, "I told you I loved you when I married you. If I ever change my mind, I'll let you know!"

This approach doesn't work in a marriage, and it doesn't work in a business—for all the same reasons. Dead air is a killer.

Excuse #3: "I don't like confrontation."

Reinforcing feedback is one of two types of feedback—the other is *redirecting feedback*, which seeks to change negative behavior or performance.

Redirecting feedback situations are often considered a battlefield, with the combatants armed to the teeth. When you enter into a feedback session with that mindset, it's no wonder you're on the defensive, with your adrenaline running high.

It's vital to remove that image from your mind. Feedback is not a fight. It is a collaboration in every sense of the word. You aren't looking to defeat an enemy; you want to forge a solid and positive relationship and help your employees grow and improve their performance. The giving of feedback—even difficult, redirecting feedback—is a gift for the recipient.

Excuse #4: "I tried it and it doesn't work."

Sometimes leaders give up because they tried to give feedback and their efforts backfired—either not accomplishing the intended goal, or even further damaging an already volatile situation. What they don't realize is that the problem was not that feedback itself failed as a leadership tool, but that the leader's use of the tool was inadequate.

Excuse #5: "I don't know how."

Ignorance is never bliss. In fact, it's a prison. And giving effective feedback isn't instinctive; people don't know how to do it naturally. Fortunately, by the time you finish this chapter, you will know everything you need to know to give powerful feedback that can transform your business.

Excuse #6: "If I wait long enough, maybe the problem will go away."

Trust us, it won't.

"That's just like you!" Frank exploded. "You always criticize everything I do!"

"Stuff and nonsense," scoffed his grandmother. "I am merely stating that failing to give well-crafted, direct, and descriptive feedback on a regular basis is counterproductive to the positive development of your personnel and is therefore detrimental to your strategic business growth."

Frank stared at her.

"What?" she asked playfully. "Do you think I haven't listened to your business gripes long enough to have picked up the jargon? Besides, what do you think feedback is other than a parent's number one tool for bringing up children and fashioning them into productive, responsible adults? I've been at this longer than you've been alive, Frankie."

The Feedback Statement

The most critical element in the feedback process is what we call "the feedback statement." We define it this way:

> **The feedback statement is the first one or two sentences spoken by the person giving the feedback, which explain to the recipient why the conversation is taking place.**

A feedback statement is similar to the concept of a first impression—the perception you form within the first few seconds of meeting a person. That first impression is very difficult to shake, even if further conversation with them proves your first impression to be incorrect.

It's the same in the feedback situation: whatever you say first is going to set the tone of the conversation and influence the emotional and behavioral response of the recipient. Anything you say after those first one or two sentences will always take a backseat to the first statements that come out of your mouth.

Feedback statements tend to fall into one of two categories, judgmental and descriptive:

- **Judgmental** feedback statements are to be avoided, because they typically do not achieve the desired behavioral changes.

- **Descriptive** feedback statements are significantly more effective in achieving lasting behavioral change.

Judgmental Feedback Statements	Descriptive Feedback Statements
DON'T . . .	**DO . . .**
SAY "YOU"	**SAY "I"**
Example: You did this. You did not do this.	*Example:* I have noticed that you did (or did not) do this.
Reason: The other person will see you pointing the finger at them and may respond defensively.	*Reason:* This is a less aggressive opening and establishes the tone as a conversation.
COMMENT ON PERSONALITY	**COMMENT ON BEHAVIOR**
Example: You are lazy!	*Example:* I noticed that you did not get the report done on time.
Reason: Referencing personality traits or characteristics will lead to defensiveness. It is also difficult to discuss personality ("You are irresponsible"), whereas it is easy to pinpoint and discuss behavior ("You did not follow up last week with the client").	*Reason:* If you are correct in your observation about the person's behavior, it will be difficult for the person to deny.
BE GENERAL	**BE SPECIFIC**
Example: You're late a lot of the time.	*Example:* You have been half an hour late five times in the past three weeks.
Reason: This will lead to argument. How much is "a lot"? How late is "late"?	*Reason:* Again, this is difficult to deny if it's true.

Judgmental Feedback Statements	Descriptive Feedback Statements
DON'T . . .	DO . . .
USE ALL-OR-NOTHING LANGUAGE	**USE QUALIFIERS**
Example: You are always rude to people.	*Example:* I have observed that once in a while you treat customers with disrespect.
Reason: Words like "always" and "never" are invitations to an argument because there are few things people do "always" or "never." They may fail to do something 29 times out of 30, but if you say, "You never do this," then they will focus on the one time they did it right.	*Reason:* Some things, such as the quality of a person's interactions with others, may in fact defy quantitative measurement. In that instance, use phrases that avoid absolutes so you can focus the conversation specifically on the problem areas.
FOCUS ON THE CAUSE	**FOCUS ON THE EFFECT**
Example: You are so lazy that you missed three errors in your report!	*Example:* The three errors in your report caused us to lose the client account.
Reason: What we believe to be the cause of the behavior is either an assumption that can be denied easily, or a personality characteristic that can result in explosive defensiveness.	*Reason:* Focus on the effect of the behavior; that is, what went right or what went wrong as a result of the behavior. After all, it is the effect of the behavior that has triggered the need for feedback. Focusing on effects rather than causes also helps the feedback to be more acceptable to the recipient.
GIVE THEM SOLUTIONS	**GIVE THEM THE SITUATION**
Example: This happened and was unacceptable. From now on, I want you to do the following.	*Example:* I was very concerned when this happened, for the following reasons. What is your opinion of the situation?
Reason: Presenting the solution outright leaves no opportunity for the person to assume ownership of the problem or collaborate on the resolution.	*Reason:* Describe the situation as you see it and ask the other person to describe it from their point of view. This increases the likelihood that you will both be on the same page.

Judgmental Feedback Statements	Descriptive Feedback Statements
DON'T...	**DO...**
GIVE UNTIMELY FEEDBACK	**GIVE TIMELY FEEDBACK**
Example: Six months ago, you really screwed up this client account.	*Example:* We need to talk about yesterday's client meeting.
Reason: The person will be blindsided and feel attacked, because they had no idea at the time that there was a problem.	*Reason:* The sooner the feedback follows the behavior, the more effective it will be.
IMPLY THEY HAVE NO CONTROL	**SHOW THEM THEY CAN CHANGE**
Example: You'll never get this right!	*Example:* I know that we can work through this situation.
Reason: If you assume that people have no control over their behavior and cannot change, you will move into the role of judge, police officer, or enforcer—all negative, because the underlying belief is negative.	*Reason:* If you believe that people can change their behavior, you move into the role of coach, mentor, partner, etc.—all positive, because the underlying belief is positive.

To help you practice giving feedback that's more descriptive and less judgmental, we've put together an exercise, included as an appendix on page 165.

"All right," said Frank, exhaling his irritation. "Then tell me how it's done." His tone was challenging.

"And so charmingly asked," mocked his grandmother. Then she smiled. "But I will. Let's start with the supposedly easy part. You have some fantastic people on your leadership team, don't you?"

"Sure."

"Name one."

"Alicia—she's head of marketing."

"Good. What are you going to tell her in her review?"

Frank lifted his hands helplessly. "'Great job. Keep at it. Thanks a million. Here's your bonus.' What more needs to be said?"

"Those are nice phrases, Frankie, but there's no substance to them. They're like dandelion fluff that blows away in the wind. What has she done a great job at? What should she keep doing? Why do you value her? How have her skills and efforts made a difference? What are you thanking her for? How do you feel about her as part of your company? If you're general, she'll appreciate the check for about three days. If you're specific, she'll be motivated to give you her best all through the next year."

Now that you have a good understanding of how to deliver a descriptive feedback statement, it's time to put everything together with two specific step-by-step processes for providing effective feedback—one process for each of the two feedback types alluded to earlier in the chapter:

- **Reinforcing feedback**, which either (1) provides recognition for regularly demonstrated positive patterns of behavior, or (2) seeks to encourage a new positive behavior that is not typical for an individual.

- **Redirecting feedback**, which seeks to change or redirect the undesired behavior of the person receiving the feedback.

How to Give Reinforcing Feedback

There are three steps to giving effective reinforcing feedback. We've seen them work time and again with our clients:

Step 1: Give a clear descriptive feedback statement

Positive feedback is *not* smiling and saying, "Great job!" That's a good start, but it's not enough, and it won't last.

We once worked with an executive who was mostly out of touch with the work going on in the office, but he would occasionally hear that a team member had done a good job on something or other. He would then step up to that team member with a broad grin on his face, slap the person on the back like a proud parent, and loudly proclaim, "You da man!"

What did the team member learn from this? Absolutely nothing!

Instead of following this guy's example, start with a descriptive feedback statement that is carefully crafted to accomplish your goal. That means you have to let the person know *very specifically* what behavior you value so that he or she can repeat that behavior in the future.

Example: "That experiment you designed was well thought out and well executed. I appreciated your attention to detail in how you designed the controls."

Step 2: Indicate the positive effect or impact of the behavior on the organization

Don't assume that people know why some action was good or important. Clarify it. Again, be specific in what happened as a result of their behavior.

Example: "Because you thought through that experiment so carefully and managed it so well, we were able to cut two weeks from our projected timeline and save money since we didn't have to perform additional experiments."

Step 3: Give your personal reaction

Now that you've made the feedback statement and told them how their action helped, it's time to share your feelings. Give your personal reaction to what you've seen or heard. Don't be afraid to show your emotion. If you ignore this step, your employee may not fully grasp the importance of the behavior and its impact—up to this point, it is just data and information. You need to touch on the emotions to drive your point home.

Example: "I'm excited about what this means for the success of our project!"

———

Now that you know the process, here's a crucial point about reinforcing feedback: *every* person needs it. Don't give reinforcing feedback only to individuals in whom you are seeking to encourage a new, positive behavior. Also give reinforcing feedback regularly to your all-star performers. Yes, they are motivated employees who consistently perform well, but if you don't recognize and affirm their motivation and performance, they will feel taken for granted and could begin to slack off. Reinforcing feedback is for everyone.

In fact, reinforcing feedback shouldn't be restricted to your employees; your external vendors and contacts can benefit from it too. Once, we assisted a client in preparing for a meeting. Subsequently, the VP of human resources called us and said, "I want to thank you for all your hard work in helping us put this agenda together. Without you we couldn't have done it. We had a meeting yesterday where we presented this agenda and got positive input. As a result, I am feeling much more comfortable about this project. Thank you both!" She did all three steps for reinforcing feedback and truly made our day.

Finally, two words of caution. First, it often takes courage to give reinforcing feedback. Leaders may feel threatened by a good performer (whether a subordinate or a peer) or may feel like they themselves should have accomplished certain tasks. In those cases, giving recognition may not come easy. However, delivering reinforcing feedback will always put you in a good light. The action itself says, "I am confident enough in myself that I can openly praise someone else."

And second, be certain that you are *sincere* in your feedback. Only give reinforcing feedback if it's well deserved. Don't use reinforcing feedback in an attempt to manipulate another person. If you tell someone that they are doing something well, when in fact they are only doing a mediocre job at best, they will know that you are being insincere.

If you use reinforcing feedback to manipulate others, it will lose its effectiveness and you'll lose your credibility. And just like the boy who cried wolf, the day will come when you will really want to use reinforcing feedback sincerely, but members of your team will be suspicious of intent.

"I see your point," Frank said thoughtfully. "Specifics are both memorable and motivating."

"Always."

"But what about the other side, Grandma?" Frank asked, and this time his tone was respectful. "What about when you have bad news to deliver?"

"The whole key to that is in your attitude and in your approach, Frankie," his grandmother replied. "Don't think of it as bad news. Think of it as news that may be a little hard to swallow but that will be good for your colleagues in the long run. Like medicine, it goes down bitter, but it makes a person strong and healthy."

How to Give Redirecting Feedback

As we mentioned previously, redirecting feedback need not be viewed as a battleground. Neither is it punitive in nature. Delivered well, redirecting feedback is a positive, empowering experience for both parties. The goal is to restore the individual to effective performance.

That is not to say that people won't get defensive in the moment; they sometimes will. Chances are, the person you are delivering redirecting feedback to will attempt various deflecting techniques: justifying themselves, blaming other people, blaming you, attempting to shift responsibility going forward, etc. This is why it is vital to have a process to follow; the process keeps both of you on track.

Here are the seven steps to giving effective redirecting feedback:

Step 1: Give a clear descriptive feedback statement

If you want to change behavior, you must begin with a *very clear* descriptive feedback statement. The other person must understand precisely what behavior is unacceptable if they are going to change it.

Example: "I have noticed that your commitment to fine-tuning graphic concepts has led to us missing customer deadlines."

Step 2: Ask why the person acted in the way they did

Don't assume you know why the person acted in the way they did. They may, in fact, have had a very good reason.

Take this scenario: You have a staff meeting with your group in the morning and review what needs to be done that day. Everyone agrees to the plan and returns to their work areas. You go to a meeting, and when you come back, one of your staff isn't doing what they agreed to do at the staff meeting. You could assume that they hadn't listened or are being lazy and attack them verbally.

On the other hand, you could say, "I thought that we agreed during our staff meeting that you would be working on the Ambrose case. Can you tell me why you're working on the Johnson case now?" Your employee responds, "The VP came along and made a special request." This is obviously a legitimate reason for the behavior in question, and therefore there is no need to proceed to redirecting feedback. But you would never have known if you had not *asked*.

Even if their reasons are not "acceptable," per se, you have done two important things: (1) you have learned something about how they think and make decisions, and (2) you have opened the door to a two-way dialogue. This automatically causes the person to be more inclined to really listen to what you have to say.

Example: "Can you tell me a little about why you handled the situation the way you did?"

Step 3: Indicate the effect or impact of the behavior on the organization

Just as you would for reinforcing feedback, state the effect or impact the behavior has had on the organization. Be specific. Make certain that the person understands the serious consequences of their actions.

Example: "I understand and appreciate your desire for excellence; however, this first stage is meant to present the client with graphic concepts only: general ideas, not finished products. Do you mind if I share with you the ramifications of missing these deadlines? We recently lost a client because we did not deliver the required number of concepts on schedule."

Include your personal reactions to these consequences; don't be afraid to use emotional words. Don't act in an unprofessional manner, but if you are angry, simply state that you are angry.

Example: "I am getting quite frustrated."

Step 4: Collaboratively seek a solution

Notice that this step is not "Propose a solution." It's "Seek a collaborative solution," emphasis on *collaboration*. Ideally, you want your employee to come up with the appropriate solution. If they do so, they will have a strong sense of ownership of it and commitment to it. Therefore, introduce this step with a question.

Example: "What do you think can be done to help you speed up your concept development process?"

Now, the employee may not know how to proceed or how to resolve the situation. Or, they may come up with a solution that is patently unacceptable and unworkable. Therefore, it is vital that you have a solution to the problem already formulated in your own mind.

However, if the employee volunteers a solution that is not exactly what you had in mind but is workable, *go with their solution*. If you start to say, "Well, that sounds fine, but . . ." then the employee will think, "Then why did you ask me in the first place?" They will also feel resentful and defensive and will not own the solution. By accepting their solution whenever possible, you keep the feedback situation positive and increase the employee's level of ownership to solve the problem.

So what if they come up with a solution that is simply not going to work? *Do not* criticize their idea! You want to keep communication open at this vital junction. Without passing judgment on the solution (e.g., "That idea is stupid!"), carefully point out your concerns:

Example: "If we do as you have suggested, I am concerned that this result might happen. How do you think we might get around that?"

In this example, you have kept the dialogue going and kept the employee involved. If the employee offers a new solution that is acceptable, go with it. If they cannot come up with an acceptable resolution, make suggestions in a nonthreatening manner:

Example: "What if we considered a tactic that involved this approach?"

By guiding the employee through this process, you are helping them become better decision makers, and you have avoided passing judgment.

This is one of the most difficult steps for most leaders. It's very tempting to say, "This is what you are going to do from now on!" However, such an approach shuts the communication lines down and often leads to the creation of a passive, dependent employee rather than an engaged performer.

Step 5: Develop an action plan

Once you have a solution you both agree on, the next step is to develop an action plan. This is simply who is going to do what and when they are going to do it.

As the leader, you have to be very careful at this point not to take on more responsibility for the action plan than is legitimate. For instance, if one of the issues involved is that the employee must have certain critical information at a certain time and you as the leader are the person who possesses that information, then it is legitimate for you to be part of the action plan. You will agree to get that information to your employee at a certain time.

However, if the issue is something like tardiness, then the only person who can change that situation is the employee. You should not get involved in doing things like calling them in the morning or rearranging schedules.

Example: "To review our discussion, now that we have determined how to proceed going forward, you will take the following actions, and I will take the following actions."

Step 6: Agree on a follow-up procedure

Once you have developed an action plan, you must agree on a follow-up procedure. As with every other step of the feedback process, you must be *specific* on how and when the follow-up will occur.

You cannot simply say, "Well, that solution sounds great and the action plan looks terrific. I think we should talk about this sometime down the road." Vague statements like this cause people to think, "Nobody ever follows up around here. I'll never hear anything about this again." Therefore, you must agree on a specific follow-up plan.

Example: "Given the action plan we have created here, I think we can see a substantial difference in two weeks as you work on the next two projects. Let's get together two weeks from today at ten a.m. to follow up. The purpose of the follow-up will be to evaluate the effectiveness of the solution and action plan and determine how far we've come."

You may find that the solution and action plan accomplished what was needed, or you may find that you were far too ambitious in the timing, or that the solution and action plan needed modification to produce the desired outcome. Whatever the case, the crucial part is setting a specific time for the follow-up and actually holding the meeting. If you say you'll follow up and you don't, it tells the employee that you don't really care and actually gives tacit approval for the behavior to continue.

Step 7: Encourage the employee

In the final step, you want to encourage the employee.

Now, it's important to understand how leaders typically act in a feedback situation. Because leaders don't like giving redirecting feedback, they try to soften it by starting with the good news and lots of compliments and then hit the employee with the great big word: "BUT."

But is a word that should never enter into a feedback situation. If you start with a compliment and then introduce the *but*, you risk erasing everything that went before. The employee will not remember any of the good things you said, only what came after the conversation turned.

That is why you start with the specific behavior you want to change right at the beginning, in the descriptive feedback statement. There's no need for the word *but*, because you have addressed the issue at the outset. The employee knows where he or she stands.

You then worked through the solution with an action plan and follow-up plan, always maintaining an open dialogue with the employee. *Now*—as you wrap up—is the time to say the good things. This positive note at the end of the conversation is what they'll remember.

To make this encouragement believable, strive to tie it into the situation and what you are expecting of them.

Example: "I have every reason to believe, based on your strong background in these areas, that we will successfully work through this situation."

=========

Is giving redirecting feedback easy? No, not even with a process. Leaders may give in to anger or a desire to be judgmental and punitive. Or they may be nervous and end up filling the dead air with irrelevancies. They can water down what needs to be said so much that the person doesn't realize what behavior is being addressed.

Giving feedback is a skill, like any other. Complete leaders master it through practice and through a careful analysis of what happened in any given feedback circumstance. But, like all the other skills we've discussed (and those we have yet to), the responsibility for effective feedback lies with the leader. The good news is that the skill can be learned, and the results are more than worth the effort.

Frank shut down his laptop and closed it with finality. "That's it. I'm calling a leadership team meeting tomorrow. As leaders, we haven't done our job well, so the change has to start with us. We're going to make this year's annual review process the kickoff for a new 'no surprises/know where you stand' policy."

"I think the only surprise, Frankie, will be in the incredible results you're going to see when everybody does know where they stand." She smiled. "Would you like some more tea?"

6

ARGUING WELL: *CONFLICT RESOLUTION*

The crash of broken china in the kitchen was followed by a string of expletives. Frank's grandmother, rocking gently in her chair, frowned but said nothing.

The disgusted muttering continued as the closet door banged open for a broom and dustpan and the shards were swept up. A tinkling sound announced the debris being dumped in the garbage can. Then another bang as the broom and dustpan were replaced.

Frank stomped into the living room. He had a hunted look on his face but conversely seemed looking for a fight, if the clenching and unclenching of his fists was any indication.

His grandmother didn't look up from the book in her lap. The silence grew awkward.

Finally, Frank said tersely, "Sorry. I broke the serving bowl."

"Forgiven. Forgotten," his grandmother replied quietly.

Frank still stood there, tension radiating off him.

Finally his grandmother looked up. "The bowl was a small price to pay for finding out what's been eating at you all evening."

Still unable to sit down, Frank took a few steps toward the mantel. He stared at himself in the mirror. "It's the PROTECH project. It's ground to a halt."

"Why?"

"Programming. Adam is VP. He's fighting me at every step. I'm ready to strangle him!"

His grandmother's brow furrowed. "I thought Adam was one of your best people."

"He was!"

"Then I suspect that he still is—despite what you're feeling right now."

Defining Conflict

What is conflict? The word itself can be used in many situations, with wildly differing degrees of intensity:

- "I'm sorry, I can't make our lunch appointment; I have a conflict in my schedule."

- "I hear Joe and Susan are struggling with some marital conflict."

- "Have you heard about the escalation of the conflict in Iraq?"

Daniel Dana, president of Dana Mediation Institute, is an internationally renowned conflict mediator known as the Conflict Doctor. He defines *workplace conflict* in the following way:

> **A condition between two people in which at least one feels angry, resentful, hostile, etc., toward the other . . . and which leads to disruption of effective work and morale in the workplace.**

Note several important aspects of this definition:

- **"At least one feels angry."** You don't have to have two people seeing something as a conflict in order to have a conflict. One person's dissatisfaction is sufficient to create a conflict situation because the relationship is disrupted.

- **"Angry, resentful, hostile."** These are all very strong, emotional words. Conflict always has an emotional component.

- **"Disruption of effective work and morale in the workplace."**
  Healthy conflict in an organization helps teams to reach new levels
  of performance, but unhealthy conflict disrupts effective work and
  morale and can profoundly affect a company's bottom line.

Based upon this definition, there is a definite difference between a
conflict and a disagreement. All conflicts are disagreements, but not
all disagreements are conflicts. People might "agree to disagree" fairly
calmly and move forward from there. People can even disagree vehe-
mently and with passionate emotion. But if progress continues, that is
still not classified as unhealthy conflict. Unhealthy conflicts are disagreements that involve strong emotions *and* that disrupt productivity and
forward momentum.

This distinction is very important for the complete leader to understand, because *healthy conflict is a normal part of a successful organization.* It's through healthy conflict that ideas are honed and refined,
problems are solved, and innovation is born. There can be extensive arguments, but as long as the communication between the disagreeing parties
remains open, honest, and transparent, that is a good thing. There can be
expressions of anger and deep emotion, but as long as there are no personal attacks, that is perfectly acceptable.

What matters most are the results of the conflict. If work is thriving,
creativity is blooming, and people are turning their creative energy into
productivity, that is the sign of healthy conflict and a healthy organization. If, on the other hand, resentment and hostility are growing, productivity is grinding to a halt, and morale is low, the organization is suffering
from unhealthy conflict. As frightening as it might be, it is critical for
the leadership team to addresses the unhealthy conflict before it does further damage.

*Finally, Frank threw himself into a chair. He put his hands to his temples
as if trying to stop the blood from pounding in his brain.*

With a long exhalation, he looked up. A bit of calm had come back into his eyes. "I suppose so. At least, that's what I've been trying to tell myself. Adam is incredibly skilled, loyal to the company, and has always been—at least up to now—a good friend. I simply don't understand how we can be at such loggerheads with one another."

"Can you pull it apart to look at it more clearly?"

"What do you mean?"

"Well," said his grandmother thoughtfully, "right now, the whole thing looks like a Gordian knot, doesn't it?"

"Yes. And I seem to remember that the only way to undo a Gordian knot was to slash it in two. But I don't want to let Adam go."

"No." His grandmother smiled. "But the person who originally cut the Gordian knot was better known for war than for peace. I think this knot can be unraveled—bit by bit. Then, when you see it for what it is, you will know how to handle it."

A Deeper Understanding of Workplace Conflict

To sharpen your understanding of conflict resolution, it is important to understand

- how people typically respond to conflict situations,
- the building blocks of conflict resolution, and
- how to have a conversation to resolve a conflict.

First, how people typically respond to conflict. The Thomas-Kilmann Conflict Mode Instrument (TKI) is a proven instrument for assessing people's behavior in conflict situations. The TKI categorizes people into five modes of handling conflict[12]:

Competing. Individuals who prefer competing in conflict situations are looking for and using power. They seek to achieve their wants and needs first. Arguments and power plays are common, and success is defined as "winning" the conflict.

Accommodating. Accommodating individuals are at the other end of the spectrum from persons who tend to compete. They are very cooperative and tend to be unassertive. They will give ground on what they need and want, even when it's not beneficial to do so.

Avoiding. People who avoid conflict will simply refuse to address the issues at hand. They will withdraw from "hot" situations, procrastinate on difficult issues, and will beat around the bush whenever possible, hoping that the problem will go away.

Compromising. Compromisers search for expediency—they want to resolve the situation quickly and relatively painlessly by seeking an acceptable middle ground. Success is defined as exchanging concessions.

Collaborating. Collaboration involves a willingness to find a mutually beneficial solution that addresses both parties' needs. Collaboration involves intentional effort and a desire to understand the other position thoroughly.

When looking at TKI's five modes of handling conflict, many people assume that collaboration should be used in all situations. But that's not necessarily the case. While each individual may tend to want to use a certain mode at all times, the fact is that all modes are appropriate some of the time. Successful conflict resolution depends upon our ability to rise above our natural tendency to use one method for handling all conflict, and to choose instead to evaluate each situation and respond to it by using the most appropriate method.

For example,

- If a situation arises where a core value is at stake, *competing* may be the appropriate response. For instance, safety regulations do not allow for collaborative conflict resolution: they must be followed to the letter for the good of all.

- *Accommodating* may be appropriate if the issue really isn't that important to you but is vitally important to the other person. You may disagree with them, but if it isn't that big a deal to you, don't make a big deal of it!

- Occasionally, situations arise where the effects of confronting the other person are worse than the effects of letting an issue slide. For instance, you may risk being fired if you challenge those in authority. In that case, *avoiding* the conflict may be better for your long-term career goals!

- Many times, a decision needs to be reached quickly in the midst of conflict. There may be no time to "step outside of the box" to seek a collaborative, innovative solution. In such instances, *compromising* is often called for.

- When you have to make a decision with far-reaching impact that requires a lasting commitment by the team, that's when it is wisest to spend time *collaborating* to find a resolution that will be mutually beneficial and acceptable to all parties involved.

It's particularly essential to understand the difference between two of these approaches—compromise and collaboration—precisely because they're often confused, with negative results for all concerned. The following visual illustration[13] can help explain the difference.

Imagine two parties in conflict with one another. The line between them represents their needs and wants:

Position A   Position B

Compromise seeks a solution somewhere along that middle line, requiring both parties to give up some of their needs and some of their wants. As a result, neither party is completely satisfied:

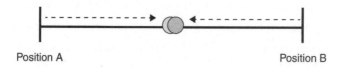

Position A   Position B

Collaboration, on the other hand, gets off that line entirely. *Both* parties choose to give up their original positions to find a third and better way—a solution that will leave both parties completely satisfied:

"Well, when I slow down and am able to think clearly, I can see where Adam is coming from—at least on some points. I don't agree with him, but I can see it. The problem is, every time I come up with a compromise position, he rejects it completely. He's not willing to bend. It's all or nothing with him."

"Without knowing the issues at stake, I can't comment on that," Frank's grandmother said thoughtfully. *"But I do know one thing—you can't always have all or nothing. Neither can you always compromise. Life is never that black and white."*

The Building Blocks of Conflict Resolution

With a better understanding of how human beings typically respond to conflict situations, we have now set the stage to examine the building blocks of conflict resolution.

Translated into a sentence, this means that conflict arises based upon what we think and feel about a situation, and about what we need and want to happen in that situation. Unfortunately, we often confuse *thinking* and *feeling*, as well as *needs* and *wants*. If we don't understand the distinctions between the blocks, we'll have a much tougher time sorting out the conflict—so let's take a closer look.

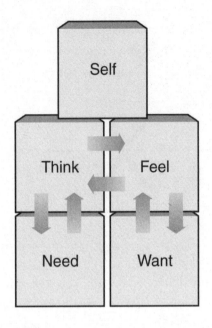

Thinking vs. Feeling

All feelings and all emotions are reactions to things that we think.

Read that again. *All* feelings and *all* emotions are reactions to things that we think.

It can be hard to separate our thoughts from our feelings about a situation, especially a conflict situation. Sometimes the thought is very fleeting or may be almost unconscious, so you may not have a great deal of awareness of it. But never doubt it: a specific, identifiable thought was there before you reacted emotionally.

After both thinking and feeling, you respond to the situation. Unfortunately—and this is key—because we are often not aware of the thoughts that have preceded our emotional reactions, we frequently respond based upon our emotions rather than upon logical thought. This is where conflicts frequently arise.

The model looks like this:

Consider the following example:

> Dave has just become manager of the graphic design department in
> a large marketing firm. He is a high-energy, proactive person with
> a passion for meeting deadlines on time.
>
> One of the graphic designers, Fred, is a very skilled artist. He
> has a low-key personality and works best under pressure. Conse-
> quently, he often appears to move in slow motion—until a deadline
> is looming.
>
> Dave asks Fred how work is coming on the XYZ Company
> account. The deadline is a week away for delivery on this major
> project. Fred replies calmly that it's all under control. Dave states
> that he'd like to see the work completed to date. Fred shrugs and
> says that he hasn't worked on it yet.
>
> Dave explodes, yelling at Fred. Dave tells him he is lazy and
> insists that Fred work overtime in order to get a good start on the
> project.

In such a circumstance, Dave's response seems instantaneous. But
there was a thought that preceded that emotional response and choice of
action. This is what really happened:

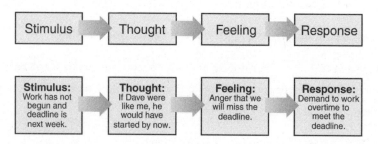

By looking at what really happened, you can see that the conflict situation could have been defused at the "Thought" stage. Dave's initial
thought—which is perfectly understandable considering his personality—
was, "If Fred were like me, he would have started by now." However, if he
had then paused and considered his initial thought, he may have realized
any or all of the following:

- "Not everyone works like I do."

- "I should find out what Fred's results usually are. If he typically finishes things on time, I should trust his work style, even if it differs from mine."

- "A lot of people work well under pressure—maybe that's what Fred prefers."

- "Perhaps Fred is planning on working late in the next day or two on the project."

All of the above would have defused Dave's emotions and allowed him to respond differently. For instance, he might have responded by

- asking Fred what his timeline for the project was,

- requesting information on Fred's work style, or

- leaving and getting more information from other sources on Fred's style and typical results and timeliness.

This drives home two of the most important points to remember when conflict is heating up:

Slow the situation down.

Determine the thoughts that are behind your feelings.

When emotions are running high, our natural tendency is to speed up. Adrenaline is flooding our system and we are in pure fight-or-flight mode. The authors of *Crucial Conversations* put it this way:

> Countless generations of genetic shaping drive humans to handle crucial conversations with flying fists and fleet feet, not intelligent persuasion and gentle attentiveness.
>
> For instance, consider a typical crucial conversation. Someone says something you disagree with about a topic that matters a great deal to you and the hairs on the back of your neck stand up. The *hairs* you can handle. Unfortunately, your body does more.

Two tiny organs seated neatly atop your kidneys pump adrenaline into your bloodstream. You don't *choose* to do this. Your adrenal glands do it, and then you have to live with it.

And that's not all. Your brain then diverts blood from activities it deems nonessential to high-priority tasks such as hitting and running. Unfortunately, as the large muscles of the arms and legs get *more* blood, the higher-level reasoning sections of your brain get *less*. As a result, you end up facing challenging conversations with the same intellectual equipment available to a rhesus monkey.[14]

In such a mode, the probability of resolving the conflict successfully is very low. This is why it is essential to intentionally slow down.

How do you slow the situation down? *Don't speak and don't take action* before you ask yourself the following questions:

- What emotions am I experiencing?

- Why am I experiencing them? What thoughts preceded them?

- Are the thoughts that preceded them reasonable? Do I have facts to support them?

- What assumptions am I working under? Are they reasonable and rational?

- Is my emotional response appropriate, based on my answers to the above questions?

Only after you have answered these questions should you decide what response or action to take. Notice a very important word there: *decide*. You should make a *conscious decision* about your next step based on logic and rationality, rather than reacting based upon your emotions. Otherwise, your action may provoke conflict rather than resolve the issue.

Need vs. Want

Another critical factor in resolving conflict is the ability to understand the difference between what we need and what we want. A *need* is something we feel we must have in order to satisfy the conflict satisfactorily. A *want* is something we would like to have to resolve the conflict, but it is not essential.

For instance, returning to the previous example, Dave *needs* to have the project completed by the deadline. He *wants* to have the work completed on his schedule—that is, piece by piece, day by day, preferably finishing early.

What he didn't understand is that Fred was intending to finish the project on time—that is, he planned to meet the real need. But Fred typically works long hours, under pressure, at the last minute—he wasn't going to meet Dave's want.

Before we respond to a conflict situation, we have to determine what we *need* from the situation to be satisfied, and what we would additionally like to have, our *wants*.

―――――

Let's study a conflict situation in detail, incorporating what we've covered so far. The substance of this case study is one we have come up against time and again during our work with companies in all industries: the battle between sales and operations.

> Mary Ann is VP of New Business Development at ABC Website Design Company. Sam is VP of Business Operations. At a quarterly meeting, tensions are running high:
>
> **Sam:** You have got to tell your salespeople to stop promising things our designers can't deliver!
>
> **Mary Ann:** The market is a killer right now. If we don't give our clients what they want, they'll take their business elsewhere!
>
> **Sam:** If we can't deliver, they'll take their business elsewhere, too! Your people are promising the world for rates that are going to kill our margins, and at turnaround times that are going to drive the

designers into an early grave. How many times do I need to tell you that we have to go through a proper process? You can't give a quote and timeline ad hoc. Company policy says that you have to get estimates for both from the design, development, and programming areas before you can submit a proposal to the client.

Mary Ann: And lose the client as we plod through your sacred process? By the time your people give us estimates, another company has stepped in and finished the whole project! And that's not even mentioning the fact that your timelines are three times as long as our competitors'!

As a first step, let's examine the thoughts, feelings, needs, and wants of both parties:

- **Sam thinks** the salespeople are overpromising to prospects.
- **Sam feels** pressured and ignored.
- **Mary Ann thinks** the company has to land clients more quickly and that if she pushes operations they will respond more quickly.
- **Mary Ann feels** irritated because the current process is wasting valuable time.
- **Sam needs** to maintain profitability.
- **Sam wants** to address every new business opportunity with a disciplined process that protects margins.
- **Mary Ann needs** to make sales.
- **Mary Ann wants** instant estimates for every prospect.

With an understanding of what Sam and Mary Ann need and want, let's explore which method of conflict resolution[15] would work best:

- **Competing** is inappropriate, because if one side "wins" all their points, the other side suffers serious losses—losses that will negatively affect the company as a whole.
- **Accommodating** is impossible, because both parties feel strongly (rightly so) about the issues at hand.

- **Avoiding** is also impossible, because the issues are continually aris-ing and causing serious problems for all individuals concerned.

- **Compromising** is not advisable, because it will leave everybody feeling somewhat dissatisfied and could potentially harm (or, at the very least, impede the growth of) the company in the long run.

- **Collaborating** is called for because the stakes are high, with long-term consequences. Everybody needs to win and feel satisfied for the good of the company. This will require finding a solution "out-side the box."

Now, will each party perhaps be called upon to give up some of their wants? Yes. Wants are not needs and should be open to discussion and adjustment. But if real needs are at stake, they *all* must be met for business to move forward successfully.

A compromise might look like this: Mary Ann gets a slightly faster proposal process, but she's irritated because it's still not fast enough to really suit her needs. Sam gets some of the steps in his proposal process cut out, so he's irritated because he feels like he is putting the company at financial risk.

A collaboration, on the other hand, might look like this: Sam comes up with solid pricing guidelines and timelines for four basic project types. Mary Ann's salespeople can give quotes on those types of projects immediately, based on that information. For projects falling outside the scope of those basic project types, a formal proposal process will still be required. But because these will be requested only occasionally, they can be dealt with quickly because people aren't being bogged down by con-stant requests for the basic project types.

"Maybe I've been going about this the wrong way," Frank said, his eyes on the middle distance. "I've approached him several times and just

suggested compromise solutions. In fact," he suddenly looked embarrassed, "I'm afraid the last time I didn't suggest it. I demanded it, rudely, to be perfectly honest."

"Never a wise move," his grandmother replied, but with amusement in her voice.

"No. It wasn't. I know that now. But since I can't unsay what I said, what can I say to get us through this mess? I don't even know where to begin!"

"You tell him the truth, Frankie. The whole truth. You leave nothing out. Then you let him do the same for you. But you don't stop there. Otherwise, it's just another hammer-and-tongs session. You have to decide together how to move forward."

"But what if we still disagree?"

"I expect you will. But since when did disagreement mean a dead stop? I disagreed with your grandfather on certain topics for thirty-eight years. It didn't stop us from having a solid marriage." Her tone softened. "You'll never agree with everybody about everything, Frankie. That's life. But disagreement doesn't have to be a bad thing if you handle it the right way."

VOMP

You should now have a better understanding of why conflicts arise and how you can help defuse them by (1) slowing your thinking down so you can make rational decisions rather than emotional ones, (2) separating your needs from your wants, and (3) choosing the right method to handle the conflict.

But the fact remains that in the heat of the moment, it can still be hard to handle a conflict situation well. Fortunately, there is a model that has been proven effective over time: the VOMP model, created by Crosby Kerr Minno Consulting (used here by permission).

First, a brief look at what the VOMP model is *not*:

When we're in the middle of a conflict-resolution conversation, the action in the cartoon can be our natural and emotional inclination. But it is essential to react calmly and professionally, and that is what the VOMP model will help you do. VOMP stands for

- Ventilation
- Ownership
- Moccasins
- Plan

V: Ventilation

V is for *ventilation*. When resolving a conflict, it is essential that each party hears the other person's side of the story. You don't have to agree with the other person; you just have to *understand* the other person.

During this stage of the process, you need to communicate both your thoughts and your feelings about the situation, and you must listen carefully to the other person as he or she explains his or her own thoughts and feelings. If he or she doesn't volunteer this information, politely and honestly ask for it.

It is important to remember that V doesn't stand for *Vesuvius* or *vomit*. You are not to explode, shout, yell, or scream. That is not effectively communicating your thoughts and feelings. Neither should you go on and on and on, verbally vomiting all over the other person. State your position clearly and concisely, and ask the other person to do so as well.

Guidelines for Ventilation:

- **Communicate your thoughts and feelings as professionally, calmly, and factually as possible.** While you are telling the other person about your emotional response to the conflict situation, you should strive to limit the actual emotion in your voice and presentation.

- **Be candid about your experience.** Talk honestly about the impact the conflict is having on you.

- **Expect to hear a different version of the story from the other person.** After all, that's part of why there is a conflict.

- **Maintain an environment in which dignity and respect prevail.** Insults or uncontrolled intensity can block progress. Refrain from name-calling and finger-pointing. If the other person can't do this, take a break and come back to the conversation later if possible, or calmly weather the storm.

- **Paraphrase in your own words what you hear the other person saying.** Again, you're not necessarily agreeing, but you are confirming your understanding of the other person's point of view. Be sure to encourage the other person to paraphrase your ventilation so you can feel heard and are sure the other person is really hearing your point of view.

O: Ownership

The next step is *ownership*. Everyone contributes a piece to a conflict. This step is where you "own"—that is, accept responsibility for—your piece of the problem.

This step is easier for some people than for others. If you have a naturally competitive nature, you will find this step very difficult. Even if that is the case, don't skip it! It is essential to the success of the VOMP process. As humbling as it may feel, admit to whatever you have contributed to the situation.

If you are an accommodating personality, however, you may find this step easy—even too easy. Be certain not to take on *more* than your fair share. Accept only *your* responsibility, not the other person's.

Just as in the ventilation stage, be calmly professional and matter-of-fact. And be certain not to make self-righteous accusations when the other person admits their responsibility! Simply accept what they tell you in the same quiet, calm manner.

Guidelines for Ownership

- **Own what you actually did and/or said:** nothing more, nothing less.
- **Don't try to resolve the conflict at this point.** If you attempt to rush the process or achieve a premature reconciliation, you will actually be setting yourself up for future conflicts on the same topic.
- **Paraphrase what the other party "owns" to verify your understanding.** As stated previously, paraphrasing helps to ensure mutual understanding.

One final point on ownership: sometimes the other party won't acknowledge their part in the problem. If that is the case, *you must move on.* You cannot control the other person; you can only control yourself. Therefore, admit ownership of your part of the situation, but do not attempt to force them to admit theirs.

Will this be frustrating? Absolutely. But take the high road. The step will still work in your favor, regardless of whether the other person responds appropriately.

The only exception to this rule is if both parties know the VOMP model and have agreed to use it from the start. In that case, you are within your rights to politely request that the other person own their part. You can state simply, "We agreed to use this model, but you're not doing your part. What do we do now?" This will increase the level of accountability on the other party.

M: Moccasins

M is for *moccasins*, from the old phrase "walk a mile in the other person's moccasins."

In this step, both parties need to express their understanding of, and empathy for, the other person's experience and point of view.

Understanding doesn't necessarily mean agreement, and *empathy* does not mean sympathy. This step lets the other person know that, given what they have told you in the ventilation step and what they have taken ownership of, you now have a better understanding of the situation as they see it. This is where you express their feelings, and they express yours.

Guidelines for Moccasins

- **Imagine what it would be like to be the other person.** What would you think and feel, need and want, if you were that person?

- **Avoid "mixing" your experience with the other person's.** Keep your focus on the other party and off yourself.

- **Paraphrase and summarize what the other person says to verify that you have understood them.** Once again, paraphrasing is essential.

P: Plan

The final step in the VOMP model is to *plan*. This is where you strive for a solution. Ventilation, ownership, and moccasins help improve morale because people know they have been heard and understood; the plan then puts work back on track. In this step, you talk about how you are going to ensure that things going forward will be different, and discuss what each of you needs and wants and is willing to do.

As you plan, bear in mind that the goal of conflict resolution is to agree on how to move forward, even though not everyone will agree on all points.

Guidelines for Planning:

- **Be realistic.** Don't make promises you can't keep.

- **Expect that you or the other person will slip up from time to time.** No one is perfect, so don't expect perfection from yourself or the other person. Be generous when mistakes happen.

- **Prepare for how you will handle things if the situation arises again.**

————

You will not become an expert in the VOMP process—or, more generally, conflict resolution—overnight. Your skill will grow and develop through practice, commitment, and motivation. But the end result—achieving new levels of both comfort and success in handling conflict—is well worth the effort!

Far from something to be avoided, healthy conflict is a contributor to organizational success. Remember the effect of unhealthy conflict: it disrupts effective work and morale. This means that effective conflict resolution can literally transform your workplace. Not only will it ease tensions, but it will release new energy and creativity into your business as you seek mutually beneficial solutions, resulting in streamlined processes, new markets, and increased revenue.

GOING FOR THE GOLD: *EXECUTION*

"Grandma, how did you do it?" asked Frank. He was standing looking at a formal family photograph on the wall.

"Do what, Frankie?" she inquired.

"Raise eight children. Keep order in the house. Manage to not just make ends meet running that grocery store with Grandpa but to actually put money aside. The whole thing." He wandered back to a chair and sank down into it.

"You mean, in a world without computers, cell phones, online calendars, and all the rest?" she said with a smile.

He grinned back. "Perhaps."

"Whether you're talking about children, keeping a house, or running a business, it's all the same: you have to stay on top of what's important. Day in and day out, year in and year out."

Execution: Bringing Strategy to Life

One of the greatest challenges every business owner or leadership team faces is executing on the strategic direction they define. Ultimately, it doesn't matter how clear your strategy is or how lofty your goals are if you cannot bring them to life.

The foundation of execution is healthy, dynamic, and proactive leadership—the kind we've focused on in previous chapters of this book. Now, it's time to explore how the complete leader builds on that foundation and gets things done on a daily, quarterly, and annual basis: how to consistently knock out short-term goals and move toward long-term goals in measurable ways.

But before we do so, take a moment to consider some critical reasons why leadership teams fail to execute:

- **Poorly defined vision for the business.** As we indicated earlier, your vision should be a realistic statement of aspiration for your business. It should be practical, specific, and targeted to help you generate the greatest value from your business. Most importantly, it should be measurable so you will know if you are achieving it.

- **Lack of organizational clarity.** Leadership teams often fail to "get the right people in the right seats" with well-defined accountabilities for each seat.

- **Lack of or ineffective use of data.** Many businesses don't have the key information they need to tell them how they are really doing. Or, they have lots of information but don't know how to interpret it to drive effective decision making.

- **Inability to resolve issues.** All too often, leadership teams don't have the discipline or courage to face the tough issues in their business.

- **Weak or nonexistent processes.** Focusing on process bores most business owners, yet building robust processes in your business will enable you to build your business more quickly and allow you to sustain your growth.

- **Inability and unwillingness to take action.** The most effective leadership teams commit to regular, disciplined, consistent goal setting and decision making. Weak teams avoid this like the plague.

- **Lack of courage.** Or, put another way: fear. Fear of change, fear of addressing issues, fear of defining roles and responsibilities. Fear is an execution showstopper.

- **Lack of follow-through.** It takes laser-like focus to accomplish even a short list of priorities. Without milestones, metrics, and effective meetings, nothing happens.

- **Lack of accountability.** A close cousin to lack of follow-through, a lack of accountability derails effective execution. Leadership teams will often make excuses for their members, avoiding hard conversations, overlooking missed deadlines, and twisting the organization to avoid accountability.

But it isn't only what a company *lacks* that creates barriers to execution. Sometimes it is what a company *has*. For instance:

- **Too many fires.** When companies are busy firefighting, they believe they don't have time to spend on systematic execution.

- **Too much adrenaline.** Some leaders are adrenaline junkies. They don't want to engage in the discipline of execution because they like the rush of the fire drill and the chance to be a hero.

- **Too much success.** Today's success can be a barrier to tomorrow's victory. If things happen to be going well without a plan, people assume they will continue on that track. They trust luck rather than skill—and in the end, luck fails.

At Makarios Consulting, we utilize proven methodologies for strategic planning and leadership development, and part of that training is teaching leaders how to execute. The execution toolset we used was developed by Gino Wickman; it's called the Entrepreneurial Operating System® (EOS®). In this chapter, we will be drawing upon the principles and tools described in this robust system (used here by permission). Gino's book, *Traction*, describes the EOS process in detail. We encourage you to buy it and read it in full.

Frank's grandmother looked at him curiously. "Was it an interest in the past that made you ask that question, Frankie, or the present?"

He chuckled. "The present. We have strategies and plans and goals coming out our ears. But the strategies take a backseat in the midst of the daily fire drills, the plans get derailed and no one seems to know why, and the goals end up looking like pipe dreams."

"Well," said his grandmother thoughtfully, "are you perhaps putting the cart before the horse? If the plans aren't working out, the problem is most likely connected with the people."

"They're good people!" protested Frank.

"I never said they were problem people. I said the problem was connected with the people." She frowned. "It's so easy to make plans and then look around and ask, 'Okay, who can do this?' But that's backward. People have to know what they are supposed to be doing on a regular basis first—then they'll be able to do their part in whatever plan is decided on."

The Right People in the Right Seats

The primary order of business in executing effectively is *not* to make a plan and dive in. That is the first mistake many leaders make. We ask leadership teams to step back and ensure that the roles and responsibilities for each seat within the organization are clear.

When roles and responsibilities are clear, everyone knows what he or she should be doing and where their accountabilities lie. Everyone understands how their work intersects with their teammates' work and with the larger goals of the company.

It sounds so simple and straightforward; it isn't.

In most companies—and size makes no difference here—two things occur that blur the lines of accountability. First, many companies do not take the time up front to define roles and responsibilities clearly. It's challenging to draw that line in the sand: "This is your job. This is not."

The second problem stems from the first. Because people aren't given clearly defined roles and responsibilities, they end up performing a wide variety of tasks in their daily work, many of which are not even close to their job description. They do these "extracurricular" tasks because the jobs need to get done, because they do them well, or because they find them interesting.

The result of these problems is twofold. First, the chain of command and the boundaries of accountability become tangled. *Everybody* does things above, beyond, over, around, and under their official responsibilities. So when it comes to execution, the question of "Whose responsibility is X?" often nets blank looks and confusion. Sally may do the task sometimes, but is it actually her job?

Second, people find their time disappearing but their task list remaining untouched. For example, one of our clients was a VP who confessed, "I know what my short list of things to do is when I start my day, but at the end of the day, I haven't any idea how I actually spent my time. I didn't get any of those things done! And yet I know I wasn't goofing off. I wasn't being a dope, or plain lazy. I didn't run out of the office at eight thirty a.m. and come back at four p.m. so I could go to a restaurant and read a book. I had people in my office. I was making phone calls that had to be made. But none of the stuff on my list got accomplished."

Blurred roles and fuzzy responsibilities make accountability, prioritization, and effective execution impossible. Therefore, it is essential for leadership teams to take a hard look at their organizational structures. They need to ask: What roles do we need to run our business? What specific responsibilities should those roles be accountable for? Should some roles be cut, redefined, or added?

It is vital to be practical and realistic in this exercise. *Everything* that *everyone* is doing should be put on the table for evaluation, with an eye toward the growth of the organization. If a task is important to the functioning of the business, it must be assigned to a certain role—officially. If it is not important to the functioning of the business, it must be cut—completely.

Once you have realistically and strategically clarified the roles you need in your organization and the responsibilities those roles will be accountable for, you are ready for the next step: to determine if you have the right people in those seats.

This takes honest conversations and courage. It begins at the top, with the leadership team evaluating their own fit for the seats they occupy. This is best done with an eye toward the roles the company will need in six to twelve months, because it forces the leadership team to define how the organization should evolve to ensure growth. When evaluating that fit, they should begin by assessing the match between their values and the company's values, *before* they look at technical skills. A strong match between individual values and the values the company has embraced can strengthen organizational health.

The leadership team should drive a similar evaluation throughout the organization to ensure they have identified the right person for each seat. In one case, we had a client where the president of the company was himself the wrong man for the seat. He was not the wrong man for the company— he was just in the wrong place within the company. He was a visionary by nature, but the president's role and responsibilities were to make sure the company ran smoothly every day. In this case, our client did not have the skills to keep operations flowing smoothly, and so his leadership team ended up running the business around him. Deep down, he knew this was the truth, but he had always denied it. Once the issue was openly addressed, he repositioned himself to a new "seat" within the company, one that we call the "visionary." This seat allowed him to use his unique skills to best benefit the company. The business, which had been flat for five years in a row, experienced 30 percent growth over the next two years.

In our experience, this evaluation usually yields a mixture of results, each of which must be addressed appropriately:

1. You have people who are in exactly the right seats. They are where they are supposed to be, and the business is the stronger for it.

2. You have people who are not in the right seats now, but reassigning them will put them in the right seats. Do it. These are good people who have been hampered by being in the wrong positions.

3. You have people who are not in the right seats, and not in the right company. They are deadwood or are creating toxic waste in the company due to disengagement. This is the time to take action. Do not

hesitate. You want a healthy company, not one riddled with cancer.

4. You have people who have the potential to be the right person for the seat, but they lack some of the skills that they need. Work with these people on their professional development.

Your assessment of the seats you need and the right people for those seats should be oriented toward what the organization should look like in six to twelve months.

"So you think I have the right people, I'm just not using them the right way," mused Frank.

"That's it. Go back to that picture on the wall. Your grandfather and I ran our store successfully, but for the first decade and more, we never had anyone except our children to help us. We made sure each one knew their chores and understood their job. With the stocking and cleaning and all the rest of it running smoothly, we could make plans to steadily improve the business. We eventually sold it and were able to fund our retirement."

"Was that always your goal?"

"Always," she assured him. "But it didn't happen overnight. And that, Frankie, is another place you keep falling on your face. You want to be an instant success, to move as fast, forgive me, as the telecommunications capabilities you sell."

"All right," he said defensively. "So I'd like to build the business to the point where I can sell it at a profit. Is that wrong?"

"Aren't we touchy! No, it's not wrong. Didn't I just say that's what your grandfather and I did? But did it ever occur to you that by focusing on your long-term goal so exclusively, you're preventing it from ever happening? At the store, we kept our goals tight—even small. Bring in a new line of soft drinks. Get a better produce vendor. Expand our convenience food selection. Little by little. One thing at a time. We always kept our end goal in sight to motivate ourselves, but we broke it down into chunks

that were realistic in terms of what we could accomplish in the here and now. You'd better start doing the same."

A word of warning is appropriate at this juncture: do not skip the steps we just discussed. Of the many companies we have worked with, the vast majority told us at the beginning of our work together something like this: "Sure, we have the roles and responsibilities set, and the people where they should be." They assumed that a quick conversation would settle the matter. In every one of those companies, just a few minutes of questioning revealed that people were *not* clear about their responsibilities, that key roles were *not* in place, and that the right people were *not* in the right seats.

Do not make assumptions about your business. Spend time in serious evaluation, holding everything—bar nothing—up to the light. You will not be able to execute effectively if people do not know their responsibilities and accountabilities.

Establish Your Rocks—Your Near-Term Priorities

Now you are ready to set near-term priorities. The EOS term for this is "Rocks." These are *the three to seven most important things you have to get done in the next ninety days* that are essential to the business and to the success of making real progress toward your long-term goals.

You have to keep your list of Rocks tight. Most leadership teams come up with a shopping list of fifteen to twenty objectives they want to accomplish. It simply isn't possible to accomplish them all, no matter how important. It's very difficult for any team to focus on twenty different deliverables. So put all the possible items on the table, and determine the top three to seven that are most important and that can be completed in ninety days.

This brings us to another point: your Rocks need to be very specific, so you know with absolute certainty when you have accomplished them. For example, a poorly defined Rock would be, "Open up a new market for our printing business." Is that even possible in ninety days? What would it look like? What is required to make that happen?

A well-defined Rock would be something like this instead: "Call on three prospects in this market segment whom we have never met before and give them a presentation on our digital printing capabilities, with the goal of securing one new customer." That is definitive and achievable, and moves the business closer to the ultimate goal of opening up a new market. Other priorities might result in a document being produced, an analysis being completed, a focus group being organized, or potential vendors being interviewed.

Once you have selected your Rocks, stick with them. Don't get distracted by the next shiny thing that comes along or derailed by the latest fire drill. Keep laser-focused on these items and *get them done*. Remember: you have already stated that these are the tasks that will help you reach your long-term goals. If you don't accomplish these near-term items, you will never accomplish your long-term goals.

Two points should be noted. First, emergencies do happen in business. That is yet another reason to keep to a short list of near-term priorities. You need to allow yourself enough open bandwidth to address unforeseen situations when they arise.

Second, you need to establish an individual "owner" and a specific date for each Rock. Ownership is key to emphasizing accountability, and a goal without a delivery date is a fantasy.

By establishing your Rocks—and their owners—every quarter, you will get great traction in your business.

Frank slowly smiled, the tension draining from him. "Yes, that would move us faster toward our goals, wouldn't it? It just seems slower at first because you're focusing on a shorter time horizon and on discrete items."

"True. But if you can find a way to see the change visually, it will keep your spirits up. We had a chore list on the wall where our children could

put stickers to show the chores they had completed. We didn't tell them that it also showed us at a glance what still needed to get done! I suspect there are more high-tech ways nowadays to accomplish the same thing," she said with a wicked smile.

The Weekly Scorecard

While achieving your near-term priorities (Rocks) will provide you with a sense of accomplishment, your leadership team should go further to track its performance on a weekly basis. Simply put, you need a weekly scorecard.

The Entrepreneurial Operating System encourages the development of a scorecard consisting of five to fifteen key metrics—financials, sales information, customer data, etc.—that enable you to track your company's weekly performance. With a well-defined scorecard, your leadership team can see at a glance how your business is performing and can focus specifically on areas that need immediate attention.

Metrics should be relevant and activity based. You want a scorecard that says instantly, "Yes, we're doing well here" or "No, we're not doing well there." For that reason, the fewer metrics, the better. As a case in point, one of our clients once developed a scorecard with twenty-eight items on it. It was a train wreck. It took too much time to review and clouded issues with excessive data. After three months, the leadership team discarded it and implemented a scorecard with six measurements. After that, they were able to make progress.

What happens when performance is translated into numbers and visuals? Simply put, people's behavior changes. If you say you want X number of new bookings in a year, or X number of widgets produced, or X number of new customers secured, and you measure yourselves against those goals every single week, you will modify your behavior to achieve those numbers.

Your scorecard will provide you with information about trends, productivity, the marketplace, and performance issues. You will have the data you need to see trends in your business, address problem areas swiftly, learn from past experience, and take advantage of opportunities as soon as they arise.

Frank laughed. "I think we have the technology to track our progress, Grandma! So here's one last question for you. How did you and Grandpa keep the momentum going, distracted as you were with eight children and trying to make ends meet?"

"By sitting together at the kitchen table every week." She gave a tender smile. "It encouraged us to see how far we'd come. Spurred us on to get where we were going."

Frank snorted. "Doesn't sound like my staff meetings! Didn't you ever have gripe sessions?"

"Early on we did—incessantly. But then we realized that was a waste of time and was just damaging our relationship and our business. So we made three rules." She stopped, her eyes looking far into the past.

"What were they?" Frank asked curiously.

"Hmm?" she said, bringing herself back with an effort. "Oh. Keep it short. Keep it focused. Keep it practical. We didn't have the time or the energy to natter on until all hours of the night. We didn't have the money to dilly-dally around with problems. We had to get things done. So that's the goal: get things done in the meeting so you can get things done outside the meeting."

The Level 10 Meeting™

Your weekly scorecard will give you the data you need and help you identify trends that highlight problem areas and new opportunities. But you and your leadership team will have to take action to address those problems and take advantage of those opportunities.

It's essential that you meet regularly with your leadership team to keep everyone on track and focused. We strongly recommend that these meetings take place weekly. This will give you the forum you need to identify, discuss, and solve the toughest issues facing your business so that you can get traction and grow. The EOS "Level 10" meeting agenda is an ideal format for these meetings. It's a unique approach to leadership team meetings that will enable you to focus the majority of your meeting time on resolving tough issues rather than reciting reports. The meeting agenda is described in detail in Gino Wickman's *Traction*. You'll learn to rate your meetings on a scale of one to ten, with ten being the strongest, most effective meeting you can have. As you get better at applying the disciplines built into the Level 10 meeting agenda, you'll find that your ratings will rise and you will get tremendous traction in your business every week. We've seen this meeting protocol work very well at all levels of an organization.

To make your management meetings effective, keep one thought in mind: *your primary purpose for the meeting is to resolve issues.* So, yes, during your meeting you will review your scorecard, update your progress on your near-term priorities (Rocks), and review your current assignments and deliverables. That should all be covered with dispatch and efficiency and without lengthy discussion. Simply identify the issues that arise when you review your weekly performance and put those issues on your "issues list." Then, the vast majority of your meeting time can be spent on resolving them. And the place to start is with the most critical ones.

We call these critical issues that hamper businesses the "elephants in the room." These are the problems that everybody knows exist but that nobody is willing to address. They are large, they are powerful, and they cause tremendous upheaval.

The temptation is to handle the little problems first, to "clear the decks" so you can focus on the elephants. Don't fool yourself. There will always be enough little problems to consume all your time, and the elephants will never vacate the premises. You have to tackle the big problems *first*. Doing so will remove leadership blockages, operational inefficiencies, toxic interpersonal dynamics, and financial waste. It will also make the smaller problems that much easier to address.

Here is how to handle elephants (and smaller animals!):

- **Identify the issue with clarity.** This can be tough. It requires honesty, and it requires trust. Don't be abrasive when it comes to defining issues, but do be direct.

- **Discuss the issue thoroughly—but only once.** Talk can make a meeting look productive when it really is anything but. Your goal is not to talk about the problem; it is to *resolve* the problem. Therefore, talk the issue through, then put an end to the discussion. It is time to move on to action.

- **Determine the best solution.** Action starts with a proposed solution. The solution does not have to perfect; it has to be workable.

- **Assign the solution to the appropriate owner.** Accountability is everything when it comes to elephant eviction. With the solution agreed upon, assign the action item(s) to specific individual(s).

- **Implement the solution for a positive result.** Now, make it happen!

Meetings aren't always about elephants. Sometimes they are about opportunities. Just as elephants will not automatically leave, opportunities will not walk into the room. Use these same steps to harness the opportunities that arise in your market. By addressing each issue or opportunity in real time, your management team's ability to achieve your corporate vision will increase dramatically.

———

Invariably, our clients show remarkable outcomes when they embrace the EOS system. For example, a specialty chemical company has increased its earnings 15 percent in the past year since the leadership team embraced EOS. They have made tough decisions to

- put the right people in the right seats,
- streamline their product offerings,
- fire unprofitable customers, and
- open the way for resources to be applied to new product development.

By running your company with this disciplined approach, you will get the difficult issues out of your life once and for all, and you will grow your business.

Frank shook his head slowly. "I swear, Grandma. I sometimes think I should make you COO!"

"I've paid my dues," she said. "Now it's your turn. And if I could do it with children, you can do it with trained professionals!"

MOVING FORWARD:
CHANGE MANAGEMENT

Frank threw open the door to his grandmother's house, his eyes glowing. "That's it, Grandma! We signed the papers today—we've acquired the programming firm!" He dropped his briefcase and gave her a quick kiss on the cheek.

"Well, congratulations!" she said. Her gaze was proud, and Frank looked at her fondly.

He accepted a glass of iced tea and sat down. "It's been a long haul," he confessed. "Negotiations, financing, legal paperwork . . . I thought the sale would never go through! I'm so glad it's over."

His grandmother frowned. "'Over,' Frankie?"

"Yep. As of three p.m. today, the purchase was complete. It's ours!"

Patiently, his grandmother asked again, "You think it's over, Frankie?"

Managing Change: A Leader's Biggest Challenge

Leading people through change effectively is the most difficult challenge in leadership. It requires all the skills of the complete leader that we've reviewed so far: varying leadership style as needed, having a sound strategy, communicating well, motivating people, providing feedback, handling conflict, and executing effectively.

In addition to being the most difficult challenge leaders face, leading people through change is also one of the most crucial skills to develop. In our experience, the number-one reason change initiatives fall apart is because of poor change management. That is, a business's leadership team may have all the information and all the processes in place to enact the change, but may not have paid enough attention to and addressed what is happening to their *people*.

Is new always viewed as bad by employees? Of course not. A change initiative is always designed to bring the business—and typically the people in it as well—to a better state than currently exists. If that's the case, why would people resist? Often, they can see that they'll be better off in the end. They should be thrilled with the change and throw themselves behind it 100 percent, right?

Wrong. Say the word *change*, and many people dig in their heels. They like the old, the familiar, the routine, and are not enthusiastic about new ideas. For many, "new" is bad by definition. The truth of the matter is that people often resist change, even when they know it will lead to a good result. That is because people don't resist change as such: *people resist the chaos that gets created when moving from the current state to the future state*. This is actually what is going on:

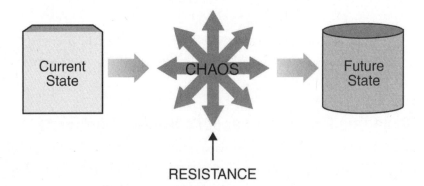

What kind of chaos does change bring? Pain, uncertainty, fear, additional work, new roles, changed responsibilities. The list is a long one. The objective, then, is to see if we can manage change to minimize both the chaos *and* the feelings people have about the chaos—and still bring about the end result we are looking for.

Frank paused in the act of bringing his glass to his lips. "You're about to burst my bubble, aren't you, Grandma?"

"Your enthusiasm and sense of accomplishment, no," she assured him. "Your pie-in-the-sky attitude, yes. But only because you may begin to see some fallout as early as tomorrow morning. I'd rather you were prepared for it."

Frank frowned. "Actually, you know, I think I had some already. The leadership team went out to celebrate the acquisition, and I figured everyone would be flying high. Sure, we've had some disagreements over this move, but I thought we'd worked through all that and were aligned. Everyone on the team did support the decision. But while Alicia and Dan were toasting up a storm, Adam was looking grim, and I caught Steve checking his watch. I don't get it!"

"Well, the moment you signed those papers, you moved from 'things might change' to 'things will change.' And not everyone approaches change the same way, you know. Even when they do agree with it."

3 Styles of Managing Change

It is critical for leaders to know how they themselves feel about change in order to be successful leaders of change. Your attitude toward change will affect how you are likely to respond to people's differing reactions.

According to John Nicholls,[16] there are three primary change management styles: according to him you're either a consolidator, an operator, or an initiator.

Consolidators

Consolidators tend to be traditional in their outlook. They want to improve existing systems by building on what is already working. As a result, they are fairly resistant to change.

As individuals, Consolidators are steady, reliable, dependable, patient, risk-avoidant, and comfortable with the status quo. In their view, incremental changes that generate continuous improvements are good, but radical change should be avoided. Nicholls points out that approximately 42 percent of the population prefers the Consolidator style when it comes to change.

Operators

Operators have a neutral attitude toward change: as long as they know what is required of them to get the job done, they are willing to be flexible. Operators are pragmatic, results oriented, easygoing team players. They operate efficiently in whatever system they are in. They are not looking to change the system, but if it does change, they'll change too. This makes Operators indifferent to risk: "It is what it is; it will be what it will be. Just let me do my job and I'll be happy." Thirty percent of the population respond to change as Operators.

Initiators

Initiators are out in front. They are excited about change and drive change. They tend to look at existing systems and say, "If it's not broken, let's break it—we can always do better!"

With this forward-looking focus, Initiators are enthusiastic people who don't like convention, are bored with daily routine, are energized by risk, and get a thrill out of the unknown. They are always seeking ways to change and improve, and they want to do so by taking a quantum leap. Some 28 percent of the population are Initiators.

You can place yourself as a Consolidator, Operator, or Initiator fairly easily by completing Nicholls's *Change Management Predictor*.[17] This is important, because this self-knowledge will help you respond positively to people who are different from you.

Is there one style that is preferable to the others? No! *There is no best change-management style.* All businesses need a mix of styles to function well. You need Initiators to spark necessary large changes. You need Consolidators to make sure that in the time between huge changes, things are steadily improving. You need Operators so that the daily work gets done, no matter what's happening in the big picture.

Consider what would happen in a company composed only of Initiators. Left unchecked, Initiators may press forward without thinking through all the ramifications of what they're suggesting, bringing serious chaos and damage to the company. They tend to throw the baby out with the bathwater, ignoring all the good in existing systems and traditions.

Alternatively, what about a company made up of Consolidators? Left to themselves, Consolidators won't make necessary significant changes. They will move too slowly to keep up with the pace of a rapidly changing marketplace. They would likely be afraid to try new things or take risks that could result in positive change for their company.

In an effective organization, Consolidators and Initiators create *healthy tension*, which leads to positive change for their organizations.

"True," Frank said slowly. "I guess I hadn't thought very much about people's feelings about change as a whole. I figured that since everyone was on board with the decision, they all felt great about the change."

"The decision to make a change and the act of living out that change are two very different things," his grandmother assured him. "Well, now

that things will change, have you thought about how you're going to make it all happen?"

Frank suddenly assumed a hunted expression. "Um."

His grandmother's lips tightened and turned down. "Let me guess. You haven't."

"We have a plan!" Frank protested.

"But—?" she prodded.

"But I think we left people's feelings out of it."

"Ah, I see. You were going to come in with all the subtlety and sophistication of a steamroller."

Frank laughed weakly.

"Steamrollers have their function," replied his grandmother. "But sometimes you need a more refined approach."

The Hammer Approach vs. the Commitment Approach

Let's assume now that a certain change has to take place in your business. You can choose one of two methods to introduce and execute the change: the Hammer Approach or the Commitment Approach.

Hammer

The Hammer Approach is a top-down change management style where changes are dictated to the employees from above. Employees are told "thou shalt": there is no room for argument or compromise or procrastination. The advantage of the Hammer Approach is that it is fast, efficient, requires a relatively small investment in time and effort, and allows you to stay in control. The hammer is appropriate when you are dealing with safety issues, when you have received new government regulations, or if you are in a crisis situation with a customer or employee. If a change is non-negotiable, then it is best to execute it without delay. Pull the Band-Aid off and move on.

The disadvantage of this approach is that people get "hammered" and can become distrustful and demoralized. You may create compliant employees using the Hammer Approach, but you will not create committed employees.

If you have to use the Hammer Approach to drive a change, there are three things you should do:

- First, *communicate*. Let people know the nature of the change, why it is being enacted, what effect it will have, the price they will have to pay, and—very importantly—the things that will stay the same (this gives people something to hold on to).

- Second, *empathize*. Change hurts! Chaos is unnerving. Be compassionate as you meet with resistance.

- Third, *listen*. Let people voice their opinions. Let them vent. The change may be inevitable, but you should always be open to hear people's concerns.

Commitment

In the Commitment Approach to change management, leaders intentionally involve their employees in all aspects of the change process— planning, implementation, measurement, and so on. The advantage of the Commitment Approach is that it is a more effective way to build employee buy-in, with the result that employees will work hard to make sure the change "sticks."

The Commitment Approach is best when you are looking to create a new norm in the business, when change needs to go beyond the performance of certain tasks to affect people's values and behaviors within the organization.

Because the Commitment Approach requires opinions, input, and buy-in—the employees literally have to take ownership of the change—it tends to require a significant investment of time, effort, and patience. Opposing views can wreak havoc if they are not managed well. The change can get bogged down in red tape and lose momentum. As a result, most companies avoid this approach, despite the obvious benefits that come from employees who are fully committed to seeing a change take place.

When employing the Commitment Approach, companies should

- keep communication flowing constantly and in real time;
- have a sponsor visibly support the change;
- use a team approach, such as a steering committee;
- engage good facilitators to help employees discuss issues openly and honestly;
- include all the players throughout the entire change process—not just in the planning stages, but also throughout the implementation;
- create "early wins" so that people can see the change is working; and
- celebrate progress as it happens, to publicly and positively reinforce the change.

The core difference between the two approaches? With the Hammer Approach, people are *informed*. In the Commitment Approach, people are *involved*.

"I guess I figured that since the change is really good for the company, everyone would be onboard and gung ho and all that. I thought they could handle a hard and fast change because they'd all be excited about it. But given my leadership team's reaction today, I'm thinking that I can expect some, ah, significant emotions from my people, other than enthusiasm. Right?"

"Count on it. What do they know so far?"

"Oh. Not much. We've kept it under wraps since it really wasn't a sure thing for a long time."

Frank's grandmother bent her head and touched her fingers briefly to her temples. She took a deep breath and looked up again. "Let me get this straight. Nobody underneath senior management has a clear idea of what has just happened and what is going to happen?"

Frank shrugged. "I don't think so. I suppose some rumors have leaked out. They always do."

"Frankie, for a successful businessman you can be appallingly naive. Of course rumors have leaked out! People are probably walking around terrified that they're going to lose their jobs."

Frank stared at her. "Why would they think that?"

His grandmother glared at him. "Wouldn't you, if you were an employee instead of CEO? Think about it, Frankie. Nobody knows what's going on except that you're about to throw a wrench into the works of your entire company. People aren't going to be happy about that at first, even if it is a positive move overall. They've got to get accustomed to the idea, and that's going to take time."

The 4-Phase Change Process

Whichever approach you use to implement change, you will see your employees (and yourself) go through a four-step process[18] in reaction to the chaos that happens between what is ending and what is beginning:

Managing Transitions

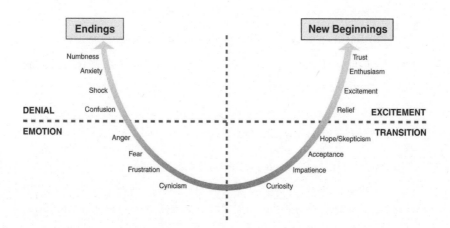

1. **Denial.** The upper-left quadrant is where we start: with denial. People are in shock, confused, and anxious. Questions abound: "How will this impact me?" "Do I still have a job?" "What are my new responsibilities?"

2. **Emotion.** As time progresses and people see that the change is going to be a reality, numbness wears off and the emotions kick in—all the negative ones. Anger: "I hate this!" Fear: "I might lose my job!" Frustration: "Why do we have to do this anyway?" Cynicism: "This is never going to work."

3. **Transition.** In the third phase, we have turned a corner. There is still negativity—skepticism, impatience—but it is balanced with positives: hope, acceptance, and curiosity. "Maybe this is going to work." "I get it; let's go."

4. **Excitement.** In the fourth phase, people are finally excited. Their overwhelming feeling is "We made it!" They may have a sense of relief. There is strong enthusiasm and a renewed sense of trust. "We're headed in the right direction. This is good for me and the company."

Now, a few key points about the universality of this progression. You will see it

- whether the change is viewed as positive or negative;
- in response to small changes as well as large ones;
- whether the change affects five people or five thousand;
- regardless of the approach you use: the Hammer Approach or the Commitment Approach; and
- in Consolidators, Operators, and Initiators (Initiators simply go through it more rapidly and reach the excitement stage faster).

In other words, *all* people go through these stages.

You cannot prevent this progression from happening. You should never be surprised when it occurs. The negative responses and emotions are normal and should be expected.

What can leaders do, then? Throw their hands in the air and give up?

Hardly! By taking the proper steps, you can effectively manage the change so as to *lessen the intensity and duration* of the second and third phases.

Managing Responses to Change[19]

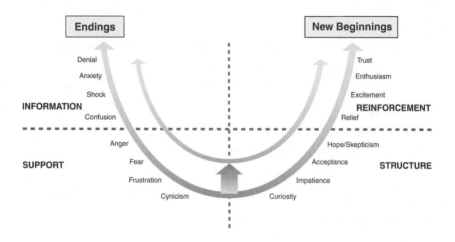

The key to managing change is to realize that while certain actions take place at the corporate level, *critical change management happens at the individual level.* Yes, business-wide communications, mandates, and directives will be going out, and that is important. But that's not change management. Change management is what happens one on one, day by day. Leaders, therefore, have to gain the sophistication to recognize which phase each individual is in and vary their leadership style to meet the person's needs in that phase.

What are the needs of each phase?

In the denial phase, people need *information.* They are in shock, they are confused, and they have a ton of questions. That means you have to communicate, communicate, communicate. When you think you have given people information overload, you have probably barely scratched the surface of what they really need to know and understand. In his book *Leading Change,* John Kotter—the renowned expert on leadership and change—states that leaders consistently undercommunicate the vision for change by a factor of 10.[20] You cannot overcommunicate during a change initiative.

Remember, as the leader, you have known about the change for weeks, if not months. You have likely already gone through these four phases! But it is brand new to all your people. Be patient: people will absorb the information at different rates. However, if you fail to communicate, the rumor mill will start up. And people never make up good rumors about change. They only make up diabolical ones!

The irony is that if you do a great job in phase one by communicating to people, you get rewarded by phase two: they become emotionally riled up, angry, upset, and cynical. Congratulations!

You now have to avoid your natural reaction: getting defensive and giving people a swift kick in the pants. Instead, people need your *support*. This means more than simply being pleasant and low-key. You need to be intentionally and personally supportive. Here is where all your active listening skills come into play. Ask open questions, use paraphrasing and reflection statements, and take nothing personally. Work at it until your people work out their feelings.

The good news is that the majority of people will work out the negative emotions. But don't expect an immediate movement to acceptance. You are now in phase three: transition. Here, as cynicism changes to skepticism and anger to acceptance, you need to provide people with *structure*. Be prepared to communicate with absolute clarity the roles that people now have, their responsibilities, who they are accountable to and what they are accountable for, the new processes and policies, etc. Structure helps people to regain their stability and find their footing in the new order.

Finally, you will get to the fourth phase, excitement. But your job isn't over as a leader! Here, you need to engage in *reinforcement*: positive reinforcing feedback, celebration, recognition, and motivation for all the ego-level needs. You have to reinforce to really achieve the new norm and leverage it. After all, the next change initiative in the business probably already needs to start!

By employing each of these behaviors, you will reduce the amount of time and disruption that the chaos of change causes. You have all you need to go from endings to new beginnings. That being said, major change initiatives may still take twelve to eighteen months. For these major changes, you have to stick it out, follow through, and create and celebrate wins along the way.

"So, some people are going to push back?" Frank asked slowly.

"'Some'?" replied his grandmother acerbically. "Try 'most,' Frankie! When your grandfather and I changed the layout in our store to move higher-volume products to the front, our employees and customers were initially confused and a bit frustrated with us. We realized we needed to give folks a lot more information about the changes and the reasons for them. We offered guided tours around the store, answered as many questions as they had, and we gave them coupons for discount credits on their favorite products. Ultimately, we created a fun game that challenged customers to find discounted products in various areas of the store, which helped them learn the store layout."

Why—and How—People Resist

As we've seen, people will resist the chaos that change brings. It's normal, it's natural, and it's going to happen. Let's take a closer look at *why* people offer resistance during periods of change:

- **Comfortable habits.** People want to maintain the status quo and avoid the pain of the transition state.

- **Fear.** The new is an unknown, and the unknown is always frightening.

- **Cynicism.** If there is a history of failed change initiatives, people are suspicious of new change initiatives because they doubt the motives of the organization and proceed to act accordingly.

- **Self-interest.** Resistance can come from the belief that something the employee values is about to be lost (e.g., money, status, power, satisfaction) and that the price of this change is too high.

- **Lack of skill.** People may resist due to a lack of skill ("I can't do this"), in which case it is the organization's responsibility to provide them with the training necessary to accomplish their new tasks.

- **Implied criticism.** The message that people sometimes get is "Now you'll do it the smart/right/safe way," implying that the old way was undesirable and their efforts were futile and misdirected.

- **Lack of trust.** Change is difficult to sell when employees mistrust management's motives and are suspicious of official explanations. Employees may remember a prior change when the benefits were oversold and negative impacts were understated.

- **Insufficient communication.** Without consistent continuous communication, people will misunderstand the need for the change, how the change will take place, and the benefits of the change. They will end up creating rumors of their own (generally negative) to fill the information gaps.

If that is why people resist, *how* do they resist? All of the above reasons really boil down to a lack of motivation ("I won't do this"), which can take two forms: overt resistance and covert resistance.

Overt resistance may or may not be verbal, but it is always obvious. You can see it in people's body language, their facial expressions, and in what they say openly. In many ways, overt resisters are a gift, because you know where they stand and you can address them at their point of need. Of course, they can also be very dangerous to the change initiative because they may go so far as seeking allies to help them resist the change and even sabotage it.

Covert resistance is—by definition—much more subtle. These are the people who smile and say, "Yes, boss, I'm with you!" in the meeting, then go back to their desks and don't lift a finger to make the change happen.

They'll never have a negative word to say to your face, but at the water cooler they whisper their discontent to colleagues.

======

Let's put this all together by looking at an example. One day, we were walking to the training room of a client with a global footprint. Three employees were standing outside the training room, and we caught the end of their conversation. One said, "Oh, right, *that*'s why we are doing this!" and the three of them burst into sarcastic laughter. We made a mental note of the exchange and went into the session.

The topic that day was change management, which was very appropriate, since the site was undergoing a change initiative. Specifically, the company was establishing a "badge in, badge out" procedure for people entering or leaving the building. We were discussing this change in the session, and we related what we had heard in the hallway. Immediately, one of the women turned bright red and put her head down. When asked what was wrong, she admitted, "Those were my people. I just met with them this morning to tell them about the new procedure." We replied, "It looks like you didn't provide them with enough information!"

This manager told her people that this was a new security procedure— nothing more. They had interpreted what she said as "You don't trust us and you think we're ripping you off, so you're acting like Big Brother." The truth of the matter was that the company had had a terrible fire at a plant in Europe; the site burned to the ground. While the fire was going on, the management was frantic because they thought four people were still in the building and they couldn't find them. Without a badge process in place, there was no record of where the people were (fortunately, they were not in the building). For that reason and that reason alone, the company instituted the badge-in/badge-out process. It was purely based on concern for the physical safety of their employees. The manager's failure to explain this clearly and well resulted in covert resistance from her people.

To reiterate, regardless of the nature of the change and regardless of the change approach that is used, you can expect both overt and covert resistance to change. But by varying your leadership style and meeting people at their point of need, you can manage the resistance, reduce its negative impacts, and move the change initiative forward.

"Then what do I do?" asked Frank. "I want this change to work, Grandma! It's good for the company—and good for everyone in it."

His grandmother narrowed her eyes. "Well, now that you've come back down to earth about the whole thing, Frankie, what do you think you need to do about it?"

"I think," Frank said carefully, "that my leadership team and I have some remedial work to do. To plan our strategy for change—and slow it down. To get our people together and communicate with them fully. To go to our new employees at the other firm and talk to them about what is and what will be happening. To make an effort to get each person on board."

His grandmother nodded her approval. "It's not too late to do that. But you said something very important, Frankie: 'each person.' You may be thinking about this change as a corporate event, but each person in your company views it very personally. So you and your team—and the managers under them—will have to take care of people personally. Person by person. There's no shortcut. Like most things in life, there's never a shortcut if you want to do something right."

Perceptions of Change: Positive vs. Negative

There are only two basic kinds of change: change perceived in positive terms and change that's seen in a negative light. *Both* require attention from leaders. You might think, "If employees see a change as positive, why are they resisting? There shouldn't be any resistance at all!" But remember, they may approve of the end result; it is the *chaos* in between that is causing the resistance.

Change Perceived as Positive

The following graph[21] shows the process people tend to go through when they perceive the nature of the change they are experiencing as positive. Note that this graph (and the one on page 158 that delineates reactions to negative change) complements and expands on the four stages of change we looked at earlier in the chapter, with a focus on patterns of resistance to change.

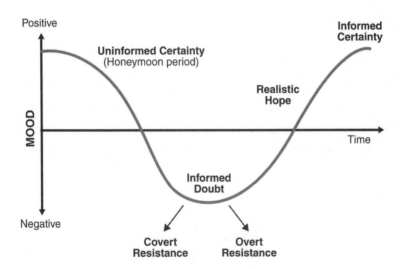

The best way to walk through this process is to give you a real-life example of a friend who made a significant career move and took a great new job that was undeniably a step in the right direction.

Our friend started out with enormous enthusiasm and confidence, loving the idea of the new job. "This is going to be great! It is the most fantastic opportunity I have ever come across. It will catapult my career to greatness!" All of this is called Uninformed Certainty or, as we say in our training sessions, "Ignorance on Fire!" Our friend was blocking out anything that suggested balance or a more realistic set of expectations.

Shortly after the new job began, our friend began to express doubts and pessimism. The job wasn't as perfect as he thought it was going to be. There was someone else on the job who was difficult to deal with. There was a demanding boss who wasn't clear about exactly what he wanted. Our friend then entered the Informed Doubt stage.

In response to his growing doubt, our friend began to resist in two ways. As he became more and more disillusioned and disappointed, he made less and less effort to be successful. He did not invest 100 percent but rather did what he needed to do to get by—a form of Covert Resistance. He also put his resume on Monster.com and began networking to find a new job: Overt Resistance.

However, after our friend experienced some success on the job, he became more realistic about it. He admitted, "OK, the job is not perfect; it's not exactly what I thought it would be. But there are some things here that are very positive. I'm in a position where I can grow and develop skills that I haven't developed before." At this point my friend was at the stage of Realistic Hope, that there was much to be gained by working on this new job.

Once our friend experienced a period of success over a few months, he arrived at the final stage, Informed Certainty, stating, "On balance, my decision to take this job was a good decision."

As a leader, when you have people going through what they perceive to be a positive change, draw upon these recommended responses at each stage:

Uninformed Certainty

- Be realistic. Communicate that this change is not a cure-all, but do so in such a way as to instill a healthy, balanced outlook—not to squash enthusiasm and motivation.
- Stay enthusiastic. Keep the energy going!

Informed Doubt

- Emphasize the long-term possibilities.
- Listen with empathy.
- Remind the person about the positive reasons for making the change.

Covert Resistance

- Engage in activities, such as focus groups, to uncover covert resistance.
- Take informal soundings from one-on-one conversations.
- Once identified, listen closely to each person who is covertly resisting.

Overt Resistance

- Educate the person on the goals and net result of the change.
- Listen, acknowledge, and take their input to heart.
- Gently challenge the resistance while affirming the individual. Try a problem-solving twist: ask the person how he or she would address the concerns.

Realistic Hope

- Reinforce positive accomplishments.
- Emphasize how close the person or team is to the future state.

Informed Certainty

- Celebrate!
- Reward achievement.

- Ask, "What have you learned through this process?"

- Prepare for the next change! (It's coming!)

Change Perceived as Negative

Now, let's turn to the process of resistance people go through when they are faced with a change that they believe will negatively affect them.

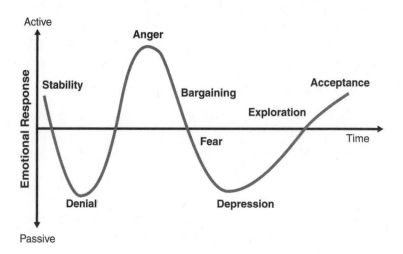

This change curve is attributed to Elisabeth Kübler-Ross,[22] who originally developed the model to discuss the grieving process that terminally ill patients experience. Businesses have embraced this model because they have observed similar reactions when change occurs at work.

To illustrate the stages that individuals or teams go through when facing a change they perceive as negative, consider the case of a large public company in the eastern United States doing business in a regulated industry. The company's workforce was nonunion. The management team took pride in the way they treated their colleagues. Unfortunately, a key way they had maintained nonunion status was by giving employees the richest salary and benefits package in their industry.

Now, the company's industry was facing deregulation and the prospect of much more intense competition. The management team realized that its high-pay package would put it at a competitive disadvantage and chose to conduct a comparative compensation analysis. They found out, to no one's surprise, that only 10 percent of jobs within the organization were competitive with similar jobs in other companies. The other 90 percent were paid at a higher level.

Compensation consultants brought in by the client designed a new set of pay scales. They recommended that people who were beyond the maximum pay for any particular job not receive increases until the market caught up with the salaries. Essentially, no one took a pay cut, but many people could look forward to a long time without a salary increase.

Understandably, this was considered a negative change by employees. They said: "They'll never do it!" "They better not try that!" "Don't worry about it; it'll never happen." These statements are examples of the Denial stage of the model.

It soon became clear to people that this was not an empty rumor: the company's leadership team was serious about the change. Employees became very Angry. They said, "I've been a loyal employee. I shouldn't be treated like this!"

At this point, a group of employees formed a representative team to talk to senior management. Their goal was to Bargain to decrease the impact of the change. They said: "I'd be willing to give up X if I got Y from the company." Employees were looking for a middle ground where they wouldn't be hurt too badly but where management could also be satisfied. However, this was not a time when any compromise was possible if the business was to remain viable.

Once people passed through the bargaining phase, they experienced a great deal of Fear. They said, "Oh no; this is going to happen. There's nothing I can do about it." Employees felt vulnerable and resigned to the outcome. This feeling of having no control over the change led to a period of Depressed feelings.

The employee team began to Explore the potential for union affiliation. They discovered that joining a union would eliminate their current pay and benefits package. They would have to negotiate new compensation terms from the ground up. In this process, employees recognized they were already making the highest salaries in the industry (25 to 30 percent more than anyone else), had more vacation time, more holidays, and enjoyed a whole host of other advantages under the current system. Gradually, they began to see exactly what their situation was and realized that in many ways they were actually ahead of the game, new pay scales notwithstanding. This realization brought them to the final phase, that of Acceptance.

Therefore, when you are leading people through what is viewed as a negative change, draw upon the following skills:

Denial

- Listen.

- Avoid confrontation and conflict.

- Reinforce the reasons for and the end result of the change.

- Rely on the goodwill that has been built up in your relationship in the past.

Anger

- Listen and empathize.

- Let people vent.

- Don't interfere unless their anger is destructive.

- Don't take the anger personally! It's not about you; it's about the change and the chaos.

Bargaining

- Stand firm on the major items.

Fear

- Acknowledge the fear.

- Determine the true source of the fear.

- Empathize.
- Increase communication to get the truth out as a reality check.

Depression

- Empathize.
- If the person is acting like a victim, encourage them to take personal responsibility to face the change head-on.

Exploration

- Provide opportunities to explore.
- Encourage creative thinking.

Acceptance

- Reward and acknowledge progress.
- Ask, "What did we learn?"
- Prepare them for the next change!

———

As you consider both of the above models, it is essential that you remember several key points:

- The stages people are going through are normal, and it is healthiest not to try to skip steps.
- People are going to go through each stage at their own speed. One person might get stuck in one phase while someone else is swiftly moving on. Watch the behavior of the people on your team closely to learn where each person stands and to help them move forward.
- Your job is not to prevent people from entering the "darker" emotions represented in these models. Your job is to facilitate them through the process.

Change management is a tall order. But with the tools and skills we have discussed throughout this book, you have all you need to lead change effectively and make success a reality in your business.

"No, Grandma," acknowledged Frank, "there are no shortcuts if you want to do something right." He suddenly leaned forward, elbows on his knees. "But we can do it, can't we?"

His grandmother smiled, and there was tenderness in her eyes. "There are only two requirements to getting where you want to go, Frankie. Wanting to get there, and knowing how to get there. You've got both. Yes, you can do it. Never doubt it for a moment!"

CONCLUSION

What Frank Abernathy learned from his grandmother throughout this book is indeed true: There are no shortcuts to becoming the complete leader. All exemplary leaders are intentional about their leadership development and are committed to putting in the hard work necessary to hone their skills in the art of influencing others. Whether it's learning how to communicate more effectively, creating an environment that maximizes engagement, or developing their abilities to execute flawlessly, extraordinary leaders never assume they have "arrived." They are obsessive about continuous learning, always seeking new ways to refine and improve their leadership capabilities. This intentional development of leadership skills is what we call "leading on purpose," and we hope that the principles, models, and tools of the preceding chapters will aid you in your quest to become the complete leader.

Those principles, models, and tools are also found in our proprietary leadership development program, The Complete Leader, from which this book grew. Over one thousand leaders around the world have "graduated" from this program, some of whom have called it "life changing." We recommend this comprehensive program to any company who is serious about developing itself and leading on purpose.

Visit the following website for more information:

www.makariosconsulting.com/services/leadership-development/complete-leader

Appendix

FEEDBACK STATEMENTS

To continue to familiarize yourself with descriptive vs. judgmental feedback statements, consider each of the following statements in turn and put a check mark beside it to note whether it is descriptive or judgmental. Some statements may be a bit gray—mark your answer according to which direction the statement leans. Some statements may incorporate a bit of the judgmental and descriptive; in that case, check both columns.

	Descriptive	Judgmental
1. I was impressed by the presentation you gave. Going the extra mile to gather in-depth competitive intelligence made the information especially relevant.		
2. You didn't run that meeting well.		
3. I notice you often criticize our clients on the phone when they haven't provided us with information we requested.		
4. When you write a report, your ideas are well organized, but you don't explain them well.		

	Descriptive	Judgmental
5. You are a positive member of the team—people appreciate your optimistic attitude.		
6. You aren't a team player.		
7. You have alienated your coworkers. You are a lazy procrastinator.		
8. I appreciate the fact that you take new employees under your wing. You have special skill in explaining our complex procedures and making them readily understandable.		
9. Two of your team members expressed confusion about the deliverables requested at this morning's meeting.		
10. You are rude to your coworkers. I don't think you have the right attitude.		
11. You often appear aggressive when some-one disagrees with you.		
12. You're a great resource on our staff.		
13. You're too indecisive. You change your mind whenever someone hints that they disagree with you.		
14. I wish all our employees were as self-motivated as you.		
15. The vice president referenced your new customer model in his recent presenta-tion. You have helped us break new ground in reaching our target market.		

Compare your answers to the answers and rationales given below:

Statement	Answer & Rationale
1. I was impressed by the presentation you gave. Going the extra mile to gather in-depth competitive intelligence made the information especially relevant.	*Descriptive:* Because the speaker references very specifically that the employee gathered competitive intelligence, the statement is very helpful for someone who isn't normally that resourceful. It explains exactly what made the behavior positive.
2. You didn't run that meeting well.	*Judgmental:* There are no specifics here. The employee doesn't have a clue as to what they've done wrong, and therefore can't correct their behavior.
3. I notice you often criticize our clients on the phone when they haven't provided us with information we requested.	*Descriptive:* The specific behavior is identified. ****IMPORTANT NOTE!**** Often, people mark this statement as judgmental because it carries bad news. There is a tendency to see descriptive statements as positive and judgmental statements as negative, but that is not the case: it is important to be descriptive whether you are addressing positive or negative behaviors.
4. When you write a report, your ideas are well organized, but you don't explain them well.	*Descriptive and Judgmental:* The statement is descriptive until it hits the word "but." Then it turns judgmental.
5. You are a positive member of the team—people appreciate your optimistic attitude.	*Judgmental:* There are no specifics here. The listener hasn't been given any data to work with, either to reinforce a typical behavior or encourage a new behavior.
6. You aren't a team player.	*Judgmental:* There are no specifics. The listener can't make any behavioral changes based upon this statement.

Statement	Answer & Rationale
7. You have alienated your coworkers. You are a lazy procrastinator.	*Judgmental:* This statement is too general. It includes "all or nothing" language and attacks the person's personality. Compare this statement to #3. What is the difference between the two statements?
8. I appreciate the fact that you take new employees under your wing. You have special skill in explaining our complex procedures and making them readily understandable.	*Descriptive:* The statement specifies why new employees like to approach the listener. Compare this statement to #5. Which statement would you prefer to hear? Why?
9. Two of your team members expressed confusion about the deliverables requested at this morning's meeting.	*Descriptive:* This isn't good news but does tell the listener specifically what is wrong. Compare this statement to #2. Which is more helpful? Why?
10. You are rude to your coworkers. I don't think you have the right attitude.	*Judgmental:* No specific behaviors are addressed. What does "rude" mean? What does "attitude" mean?
11. You often appear aggressive when someone disagrees with you.	*Descriptive and Judgmental:* The words "often" and "appear" are descriptive language (but weak), whereas the word "aggressive" is judgmental because it refers to a characteristic of the person's personality, not a specific behavior.
12. You're a great resource on our staff.	*Judgmental:* This is positive feedback, but it is judgmental because it lacks specifics. How believable is it? What does it tell the listener? Compare this statement to #8. Which is more believable? More satisfying to hear?
13. You're too indecisive. You change your mind whenever someone hints that they disagree with you.	*Judgmental:* This addresses personality characteristics.

Statement	Answer & Rationale
14. I wish all our employees were as self-motivated as you.	*Judgmental:* This statement is pleasant to hear but doesn't identify specific positive behaviors.
15. The vice president referenced your new customer model in his recent presentation. You have helped us break new ground in reaching our target market.	*Descriptive:* This statement both indicates a specific behavior and identifies the positive result of the behavior.

NOTES

1 James M. Kouzes and Barry Z. Posner. *The Leadership Challenge*. San Francisco: John Wiley & Sons, 1995, p. 30.

2 This section summarizes the Blake & Mouton Model, which is described in depth in their book *The Managerial Grid*. Houston, TX: Gulf Publishing Company, 1964. Used here with permission.

3 Joan Magretta. *Understanding Michael Porter: The Essential Guide to Competition and Strategy*. Boston, MA: Harvard Business Review Press, 2012, p. 17.

4 Ibid.

5 To learn more about the Net Promoter score, read *The Ultimate Question* by Fred Reichheld (Harvard Business School Press).

6 Joan Magretta. *Understanding Michael Porter: The Essential Guide to Competition and Strategy*. Boston, MA: Harvard Business Review Press, 2012, pp. 28–29.

7 Gallup, Inc. "State of the American Workplace Report 2008–2010." 2010, p.4.

8 Clint Swindall. *Engaged Leadership*. Hoboken, NJ: John Wiley & Sons, Inc., 2007, p.4.

9 Source: James Howard, Management Research Consulting (study conducted for Ziglar Training Systems), 2003.

10 Brian Brim. "Debunking Strengths Myth #2: Why Taking a Strengths-based Approach Isn't as Easy as It Seems." Gallup Management Journal Online, January 10, 2008, pages 1–3; Jennifer Robison. "The Business Benefits of Positive Leadership: Finding the Connection Between Productivity and Positive Management Behavior." Gallup Management Journal Online, May 10, 2007, pages 1–5.

11 Ken Blanchard. *Heart of a Leader*. Colorado Springs, CO: David C. Cook, 2007, p. 14.

12 Modified and reproduced by special permission of the Publisher, CPP, Inc., Mountain View, CA 94043, from the Thomas-Kilmann Conflict Mode Instrument by Kenneth W. Thomas & Ralph H. Kilmann. Copyright 1974, 2002, 2007 by CPP, Inc. All rights reserved. Further reproduction is prohibited without the Publisher's written consent.

13 Modified and reproduced by special permission of the Publisher, CPP, Inc., Mountain View, CA 94043, from the Thomas-Kilmann Conflict Mode Instrument by Kenneth W. Thomas & Ralph H. Kilmann. Copyright 1974, 2002, 2007 by CPP, Inc. All rights reserved. Further reproduction is prohibited without the Publisher's written consent.

14 Kerry Patterson, Joseph Grenny, Ron McMillan, and Al Switzler. *Crucial Conversations*, 2nd ed. New York: McGraw-Hill, 2011, p. 5.

15 Modified and reproduced by special permission of the Publisher, CPP, Inc., Mountain View, CA 94043, from the Thomas-Kilmann Conflict Mode Instrument by Kenneth W. Thomas & Ralph H. Kilmann. Copyright 1974, 2002, 2007 by CPP, Inc. All rights reserved. Further reproduction is prohibited without the Publisher's written consent.

16 John Nicholls. *Change Management Predictor*. 2002. Reproduced with permission by Organizational Learning Tools, Inc.

17 If you would like to give yourself a comprehensive test, we recommend John Nicholls's *Change Management Predictor*, available through Organizational Learning Tools, Inc.

18 Copyright © 1991 William Bridges, Susan Bridges. Reprinted by permission of Da Capo Lifelong Books, a member of the Perseus Books Group.

19 Copyright © 1991 William Bridges, Susan Bridges. Reprinted by permission of Da Capo Lifelong Books, a member of the Perseus Books Group.

20 John P Kotter. *Leading Change*. Boston, MA: Harvard Business Review Press, 1996, p. 9.

21 This model is based on Daryl R. Conner's Organizational Change Model in *Managing at the Speed of Change: How Resilient Managers Succeed and Prosper Where Others Fail*. New York, NY: Random House, 1992, 2006.

22 This model is based on the work of Elisabeth Kübler-Ross, *On Death and Dying*. New York: Scribner, 1970, 1997.

INDEX

ABOUT THE AUTHORS

Timothy I. Thomas began his work in leadership consulting in 2003 as a natural outgrowth of his educational background and his lifelong commitment to helping others succeed. He is a 1987 magna cum laude graduate of the University of Akron and holds two master's degrees: a master of divinity from Princeton Theological Seminary (1990), and a master of science in training and organizational development from Saint Joseph's University in Philadelphia (2002).

As the founding partner of Makarios Consulting, Tim has helped to transform organizations since 1998, working as a leadership development trainer, executive coach, and change management expert. Tim has extensive expertise in training design and delivery, executive coaching, performance consulting, team development, and 360-degree appraisal processes. He brings to his clients a complete understanding of corporate culture and business processes as well as keen financial acumen, having himself been a vice president at two international banking institutions.

Known for his highly energetic and engaging facilitation style and his strong commitment to helping his clients realize their full potential, Tim has trained or coached hundreds of leaders in the art of influencing others to achieve extraordinary results in business and in life.

Tim is the coauthor of *HeadTrash: Cleaning Out the Junk That Stands Between You and Success.*

Charles "Rip" Tilden joined Makarios Consulting as a partner in 2009, bringing with him more than thirty-five years of leadership experience as a senior executive in a wide range of public and private companies. He is highly regarded as an effective team builder and leader with a proven ability to lead change, grow organizations, and deliver strong results in intensely competitive industries.

Rip has led organizations with business operations in the United States and with strong customer footprints in Europe and Asia. He is known for integrity, outstanding communication skills, and a consistent record of successfully executing strategic vision to grow enterprise value.

Rip earned his BA from DePauw University and his MBA from the University of Chicago (1982) and is a project faculty member at the Wharton School of the University of Pennsylvania.